Lazy Thoughts of a Lazy Girl

W0038279

Lazy Thoughts of a Lazy Girl

Jenny Wren

ET REMOTISSIMA PROPE

Hesperus Classics

Hesperus Classics
Published by Hesperus Press Limited
4 Rickett Street, London SW6 1RU
www.hesperuspress.com

First published in 1891
First published by Hesperus Press Limited, 2010

Whilst the text of Lazy Thoughts of a Lazy Girl *has been reproduced as per the original edition, the opinions expressed within it by no means reflect those of the publisher.*

Foreword © Jenny Éclair, 2010

Designed and typeset by Fraser Muggeridge studio
Printed in Jordan by Al-Khayyam Printing Press

ISBN: 978-1-84391-168-5

CONTENTS

FOREWORD

First published in 1891 as a female riposte to Jerome K. Jerome's *Idle Thoughts of an Idle Fellow*, the identity of the author of Lazy Thoughts of a Lazy Girl is unknown. 'Jenny Wren' is obviously a pseudonym but the name could hardly be more apt. The wren is the second smallest bird in the UK, by nature a humorous bird (it is partial to cheese) with a shrill piping voice belying its size: a characteristic shared perhaps by our writer? We are told that the author was only five feet four inches, a measurement she despised – but what she lacked in height, she more than made up for in personality.

One can speculate endlessly about who the 'Wren' was (I have a horrid suspicion that she might have been none other than Jerome K. Jerome himself, the style is so comically fluent, though I hope there is no evidence to back this cynical theory up!). But regardless of her identity, the book is a fabulous insight into the day to day morals, manners and mindset of the Victorian middle class.

Anything but lazy, this book fizzes throughout with a fantastic energy as Wren offers us a thorough dissection of a world that is in some respects very removed from our own – and in others weirdly relevant to young women today. Time moves on but we turn in circles, and women in particular, seem to confront the same problems, generation after generation. All the subjects that can still be found in current women's magazines – politics, country versus town, children and dogs, amongst other topics – are efficiently dealt with by Ms Jenny Wren. It is relationships and the futility of finding a soul mate, though, which perhaps provide the juiciest worm for this particular bird to chew on.

Written from the viewpoint of a happily unmarried under twenty-five year old female, who is effortlessly wise and grumpy beyond her years, we are treated to an insider guide to life amongst the respectable pre 'chattering classes' of the late nineteenth century.

Wren is fantastically caustic and dismissive of both old and new manners. She disparages the pointlessness of some modern habits, and where necessary, pours scorn on traditional customs that seem to have been passed on for very little reason. The whole notion of socialising, the 'at homes', the 'afternoon teas,' the dances, all come under her microscopic eye.

Although much of nineteenth-century society is exposed as silly, what is both amusing and interesting is that, although we are more than a century away from much of the pettiness of Victorian morality, we have simply replaced their silly habits with equally silly habits of our own. We might be more liberated in many ways but it is almost reassuring to realise that some things never change, snobbery just takes on different disguises throughout the years and we are as much lumbered now with class and position as we ever were.

A lot of the charm of the book is about recognising the past in today. Crabby maiden aunts are eternally crabby, Uncles are still making 'villainous puns', and Christmas is as difficult as it always was. Nothing is safe from or sacred to the Wren.

Amidst the wry tone there are many intriguing and varied personal details. She admits to a tea dependence; she mentions Wilkie Collins, himself an irrepressible bohemian, defiant of the respectable world. (Collins was averse to marriage to the extent that he divided his life between two women, making an honest woman out of neither of them, but splitting his estate between both of them and their families upon his death.) Jenny Wren, like Collins, is suspicious of marriage, not being able to see what was in it for either sex. Ever the tomboy, one gets the feeling that had she been born a man, she would have been loathe to give up her freedom for some simpering woman; indeed, she refers to men 'saddling' themselves with wives. She is fabulously caustic about the romance of love, and at times her voice could be that of a twenty-first century post-feminist feminist.

Wren herself was obviously well educated, but only in the way that women were educated back in the nineteenth century – so although she could speak a little French and German, she laments that when she has bills to pay, she has less chance of making money than a domestic. She attempts to sell her paintings, to transcribe manuscripts and has an unsuccessful stab at writing 'tales', all to no avail. In terms of earning her own living, Wren admits she would have been better off being brought up as a 'scullery maid'.

Brilliantly observant of class, sex and manners, Wren is at her best when discussing the failings of men. It is here that her skill at description really comes into play – as when she describes the mouth of a certain gentleman being so wide that he could have 'whispered in his own ear had he wished'.

But what is most wonderful about this book is the even sidedness of her arguments. Wren refuses to let women off the hook – she is as critical of their weaknesses and pettiness as she is of the vanity of men. She is also the first to laugh at herself. Wisely, though, she is only self-deprecating up to a point, quoting Shakespeare's observation that 'self love is not so vile a thing as self neglect'.

Witty and scathing, *Lazy Thoughts of a Lazy Girl* is still a delicious read over a century after it was written. But it is more than just a good laugh. Jenny Wren has created a heroine of her day – a fabulous ballsy commentator on a changing society – and one who deserves to be read for a very long time to come.

– *Jenny Éclair, 2010*

Lazy Thoughts of a Lazy Girl

(Sister of that *Idle Fellow*)

1
ON LOVE

Love is of man's life a thing apart;
'Tis woman's whole existence.[1]

So sings the poet, and so agrees the world. Humiliating as it is to make the confession, it is undeniably true. 'Men and Dress are all women think about,' cry the lords of creation in their unbounded vanity. And again, we must submit – and agree – to the truth of the accusation; at any rate, in nine cases out of ten. Fortunately I am a tenth case; at least, I consider myself so. I don't dispute the 'dress' imputation. I am very fond of dress. Nearly as fond of it as the twenty-year-old youth, and saying that, I allow a good deal. But very few of my thoughts are given to the creature 'man'! I do not think him worth it. As my old nurse used to say, 'I never 'ad no opinion of the sex!'

Do not conclude, however, because of my statement that I am a disappointed, soured old maid, for I am nothing of the sort. I am on the right side of twenty-five, and I have never been crossed in love; indeed, I have never even experienced the tender passion, and only write from my observations of other people; thus taking a perfectly neutral ground in speaking of it at all.

One never hears that Adam fell in love with Eve, or that Eve was passionately attached to Adam. But then, poor things, they had so little choice – it was either that or nothing. Besides, there was no opposition to the match, so it was bound to be rather a tame affair. For my part, I pity Eve, for Adam was, I think, the very meanest of men. When he was turned out of the garden, what a wretch he must have felt himself! And how he must have taunted his poor wife! Weak men are always bullies.

But '*revenons à nos moutons*,'[2] I am wondering who was the first person to fall in love! Cain *might* have done so with his mysterious wife; history does not say. But certainly there is always some attraction in mystery, so such a thing is possible. I wonder whence that extraordinary woman sprang![3]

Neither do we hear much of Noah's domestic experiences, but I should conclude on the whole that they were not happy. No man could be endured for forty days shut up in the house, no business to go to, nothing to do, always hanging about, his idle hands at some mischief or other, and last, but not least, a diabolical temper, displayed at every turn! Why, I cannot endure one for a week! My only wonder is that the female population of the Ark did not rise up in a body and consign their lords and masters to the floods.

Poor men, they deserve a little of our pity too, perhaps; for if Mrs Noah and her daughters-in-law at all resembled their effigies in the Noah's Arks of the present day, they were women to be avoided, *I* think.

So that, after all, it must have been Jacob who set such a very foolish example; because we could not count Isaac, his being so extraordinary and isolated a case, when he fell in love with his own wife!

Therefore I think we owe Jacob a great many grudges. He was the inventor of the tender passion, and since his time people have begun to follow his example long before they come to years of discretion, simply because their parents did so before them, and they think they are not grown up, that they are not men, unless they have some love affair on hand.

Some get married at once, some wait a long time, and some do not marry at all. These last are, I think, generally the happiest, for this so-called love lasts for only a very short time, and neither husband nor wife is long before they console themselves with someone else's affection to make up for what is wanting on the part of the other.

Of course I am speaking generally. As far as I can see, the majority act thus, though I am glad to say that many and various are the exceptions. It was only the other day I came across our washerwoman and asked her how she and her husband got on together. He used to be a drunkard, and used her cruelly, but two years ago he took the pledge and, what is more, he kept it. 'Lor', mum,' she exclaimed fervently, 'we draws nearer every day!' I am afraid not many husbands and wives could say the same.

People are so anxious to marry too. I cannot understand them, men especially. They have their clubs, they are entirely independent, and can go home as late as they please without being questioned as to their whereabouts. And yet, as soon as they can, they saddle themselves with a wife, who requires at least half the money – they have never found sufficient for themselves alone – besides a great deal of looking after!

Women, on the contrary, are different. They have to make some provision for the future, so to speak. How do you like it, O men, the idea that you, with your handsome personages and fascinating ways, are used only as a kind of insurance office? This is the case very often, however, though you may not know it!

Yet others pursue the god Hymen merely for the sake of being married. As soon as they leave the schoolroom, sometimes before, they begin their search for a husband, and look out for him in the person of every man they meet. No matter who it is so long as they are married before So-and-So, and can triumph over all their friends.

It must be said for men that they are falling off in the marrying line. This is not nearly such a proposing generation as the last. Then they married much younger and seemed to propose after a few days' acquaintance. No, this is a more cautious age altogether. Men look round carefully before they make their choice. They sample it well, they watch it in the home circle, they watch it abroad, they watch it with other men, and finally come to the conclusion that it is worthy to be allied to their noble selves, or they don't!

Another thing. Men of the present day are so direfully afraid of a refusal! So fearful are they that, rather than risk one, they give up many chances of happiness.

They expect that a girl should show her feeling towards them, before they come to the point. But you must remember that girls also have to be cautious, and a few – I acknowledge it is only a few – would rather die than show they cared for a man who after all might only 'love and ride away'.

Not that I altogether blame man in this respect. I always admire pride and am afraid I should not care for a refusal myself. I am intolerant of it even in the smallest matters!

It is curious how men run in grooves. The same style of man nearly always marries the opposite type of girl. I mean that the intellectual, the clever, invariably choose the insipid brainless girl. Pretty, she may be, but it is in a doll-like way, with not a thought above her household. You would have imagined that such men would require some helpmeet, in the fullest sense of the word; with a brain almost as quick as their own. But such a choice occurs very seldom.

Again, why is it that little men always select the very tallest women they can find? You would think that a man would hesitate to show off his meagre inches to such bad advantage. But these pygmies appear to enjoy the contrast. It is evidently quantity they admire, not quality.

I dare say a good deal of what I have written sounds very cynical, but perhaps my experience has been unfortunate, therefore you must forgive me; certainly it is sometimes very difficult to distinguish between the real thing and its successful counterpart.

Parents are greatly at fault in the issues of the matrimonial market. After all these centuries of experience, you would give them credit for more tact than they possess. Any match they do not desire, they oppose at once, and thereby set alight all the contradictory elements in your nature. If Laban had been less obstinate, and had consented to an alliance between Jacob and Rachel from the first, provided Leah was left behind to look after him, the latter would immediately have been endowed with attractions innumerable to Jacob, tender eyes and all!

Nowhere is there such a fertile soil for love as opposition!

On the other hand, if parents wish to encourage a match, young people are thrown together as much as possible. However big the gathering, you are somehow always paired off with the eligible party until you grow to loathe the man and would sooner become an 'old maid' than marry him.

Parents have a bad time altogether, I am afraid. Their nice little plans are so nearly always upset by their ungrateful children, and then they have to be continually looking after their brood. I knew one mother who used to take her daughters on the pier and lose sight of them at once, as they paired off with their he-acquaintances. Do what she would, she could not find them again, so many were the nooks and crannies near at hand. Finally she had recourse to the Camera Obscura, and, with the help of the views set before her there, she found the missing girls! 'We never can escape her now,' they told me in mournful tones, after her fatal discovery.

Girls are degenerating sadly, it is said. They are getting too masculine, too independent, too different from man's ideal –

the modest little maid who sits at home and mends her husband's socks.

I do not dispute the fact. They *are* degenerating. Neither, though I dislike the ideal specimen, and have a contempt for her, do I stand up for the other extreme. I have a horror of fast masculine girls and agree with all that is said against them. Nevertheless, I do not consider men have any right to complain, as they are the chief cause of the deterioration of our sex.

Everyone knows that a girl thinks more of a man's opinion than that of anyone else. If he applauds, then she is satisfied. She does not consider it ignominy to be termed 'a jolly good fellow!' She gets praise, and in a way admiration, when she caps his good stories, smokes and drinks brandies and sodas. Unfortunately she does not hear herself discussed when he is alone with his friends, or perhaps she would be more cautious in her manners and conversation for the future, for this is not the kind of girl who is

Rich in the grace all women desire,
Strong in the power that all men adore.[4]

2
ON BILLS

BILLS! BILLS! BILLS! Detestable sound! Obnoxious word! Why were such things ever invented? Why are they sent to destroy our peace of mind?

They always come, too, when you are expecting some interesting letter. You hurry to meet the postman, you get impatient at the length of time he takes to separate his packets (I sometimes think these men find pleasure in tantalising you and keep you waiting on purpose), and when he at last presents you with your long-expected missive, behold, it turns to dust and ashes in your hand – metaphorically speaking, of course.

It is a pity such a metamorphosis does not occur in reality; for the wretched oblong envelope, with the sprawly, flourishy writing, so unmistakably suggests a bill that you – well, I do not know what *you* do on such an occasion; *my* letter, which I have been so anxious to obtain, is flung to the other side of the room.

How is it that bills mount up so quickly? You buy a little ribbon, a few pairs of gloves, some handkerchiefs – mere items in fact, and yet when quarter day[5] comes round you are presented with a bill a yard long which, as your next instalment of money is fully mortgaged, is calculated to fill you with anything but extreme joy.

Why are the paths leading to destruction always so much easier of access than any other? It takes so much less time to run up a bill, it is so much simpler to say, 'Will you please enter it to my account?' than to pay your money down. First the bill has to be added up, and, strange as it may seem, these shop people appear to take *hours* over a simple addition sum. 'Eight and elevenpence halfpenny if you please, ma'am.' Of course you have not enough silver and so are obliged to wait for change. Then someone has to be found to sign. Altogether it takes quite five minutes longer paying ready money; and think how five minutes after each purchase would mount up in a day's shopping! I should say that, on an average, you might call it two important hours regularly thrown away. 'And a good job, too,' perhaps our fathers, husbands and brothers would say. But, then, you see, they are Philistines and do not understand.

But though we suffer somewhat at the hands of these shop people, I think in their turn they have to endure a great deal more from their customers. I have seen old ladies order nearly the whole shop out, turn over the articles and, having entirely exhausted the patience of their victims, say, 'Yes – all very pretty – but I don't think I will buy any today, thank you,' and they move off to other counters to enact the same scene over again. Selfish old things!

I was dreadfully hard up a short time ago, and of course my bills were ten times as big as usual. I had no money coming in and could not conceive how I was to meet my debts.

It is astonishing, when you come to try it, how few paths there are open for poverty-stricken ladies to make a little money, especially when your object is to keep your difficulties a secret from your mankind. I tried every imaginable way without success. What is the good of having an expensive education, of being taught French and German – neither of which languages, by the way, when brought to the test, a girl can ever talk, or at any rate so as to be understood? What is the good of it all, I say, when you want to turn your hand to making a little money? I felt quite angry the other day when, our cook being ill, we had a woman in to take her place. Fifteen shillings a week she made! She, who had had little or nothing spent on her education, could yet make more shillings in a week than I could pence! I began to wish I had been brought up as a scullery maid.

I can paint rather well, but what are the advantages of art compared to those of cookery? Many and many a shop I went into, carrying specimens of my talent and asking the owners if they would employ me to decorate their tambourines, bellows &c. But no, they all had their own especial artists and were quite suited. It is such a dreadfully humiliating business. At the first place I could have slain the man for his impertinence in declining, and I left the shop with a haughty mien and my head in the air. But I grew accustomed to it in time, and even used to try a little persuasion, which, however, proved of no avail. One man offered to exhibit my wares (I felt quite like a pedlar going his rounds), and through him I sold two tambourines. Then who so proud as I, though my profits only came to a few shillings? However small, the first taste of success is always exhilarating, though indeed my confidence did not last long, for this was my first and last experience of money-making in the painting line.

I used to search the sale and exchange columns of the papers, and found once that someone wanted music transposed. I wrote directly, offering my services and charging a shilling per piece or song. For a wonder I was successful, for the person answered, asking for a specimen of my skill, which she was pleased to say would do very well.

How her letters used to amuse me! She must have been a rather incapable singing mistress, I think. Her letters, though properly spelt, were written in an uneducated hand and she addressed me as if I were a servant. She used to give me very little time in which to transpose her songs and insisted on their being finished when she wanted them. Sometimes I was quite tired out, for copying music is not a thing to be done in a hurry.

Somehow, our negotiations did not last long. Whether I grew careless, or she found others to do the work cheaper, I do not know, but she suddenly withdrew her custom and I have never heard from her since.

My next venture was tale writing. Who has not tried this most unsatisfactory method? It is a tremendously anxious time when your first effort is sent out. What a lot of money you expect to obtain for it! You do not intend to be unprepared, so you spend every penny in your mind beforehand. Then there are the honour and glory of it! You will hear everyone talking of the cleverly written tale and wondering who is the gifted author!

What made me more hopeful was the possession of a cousin who was very successful in this line. Indeed, she has reached the three-volume stage by now and is beginning to be quite well known. I have lost my interest in her, however, since she took me and my family off in one of her books. It is such an easy thing to do. You only have to find out a person's peculiarities – and everyone has a peculiarity! – and overdraw them a little. My sisters and I, I remember, figured as three brainless, fast girls, which would only have amused us had she left the rest of the family alone. It is a foolish thing to do, for besides nearly always giving offence it is not by any means an evidence of good taste.

It is much more difficult to write a tale than some people think; you get in such hopeless tangles sometimes. People you kill off in the first chapter, you sadly need in the last. Then, when you are finishing up, there are so many people to get rid of that you are obliged to dispatch them in a bunch with an explosion, or something equally probable – three or four strangers as a rule, who have never seen each other before, but who considerately assemble in one place to meet their doom. Then the last pages will never fit in with the first. Your meek but lovely heroine at the beginning has been transformed into a beautiful vixen as you near the end and is quite unrecognisable. The worst parts of all are the sensational ones. You think you have worked your hero up to a pitch of fiery eloquence, while his fiancée is dying in agony close by, and when you complacently turn to read over the passage, you find his words imply no more sorrow than they would at the death of a relative from whom he had expectations, or – a mother-in-law!

It is rather a difficult matter in a large family to keep your actions a secret. Obtuse as most men are, with things going on right under their eyes, it is not easy to baffle them when once their curiosity is roused. And yet curiosity is always imputed exclusively to women! Though Eve *was* the first to taste the apple, Adam had no intention of being behindhand. I know a man who always manages to get down to breakfast five minutes before the rest of his family for the purpose of examining the correspondence all round.

Fortunately I managed to escape from these inquisitive eyes, for I met the postman myself when he brought back my first tale. It was returned with the editor's 'compliments and thanks', coupled with the regret that he could not make use of my contribution.

I don't know that I ever felt such keen disappointment as when that tale came back from its first visit. I had hoped so much from it and had been so confident of its success. It depressed me for some time and it was long before I ventured upon anything in the literary way again. But habit is second nature, they say, so after that and other tales had been the round of all the magazines and returned to their ancestral home, decidedly the worse for their outings (change of air evidently does not agree with MSS), they affected me no more than the receipt of a tradesman's circular. In fact I grew quite to welcome them as old friends, and no one would have been more astonished than I had they been converted into l.s.d.[6]

Apparently I am not cut out for literary work. I have not sufficient imagination, nor am I sceptical enough for this fanciful and scientific age. The world only cares for impossible adventures and magic stories, or stories which undermine their religion or upset it altogether, and I am not clever enough for this.

Of course, in my pecuniary need I did not neglect to employ a 'chancellor of the exchequer', as Miss Mathers calls her; a 'wardrobe keeper', as she terms herself. Indeed, I employed two or three, and so had plenty of opportunities of observing the type.

These women certainly vary in the way they carry on business, but very rarely do they vary in appearance. For the fattest, ugliest, oiliest old creatures to be found anywhere, commend me to a chancellor! I pause in astonishment sometimes, and wonder how they have the strength to carry so much flesh about with them.

The first one I engaged possessed a complexion of a glowing yellow, like unto the petals of an allamanda. She carried on the business in a too independent way altogether. She would take up my garments, look them over with a contemptuous sniff (what eloquence there is in a sniff!) and then begin to talk of the 'ilegant costoomes she 'ad 'ad lately of Lady —, of the 'ansome silks and furs purchased from the Countess of —' &c. It was cunningly and knowingly done. Immediately, as was intended, my productions began to lose value in my eyes, in contrast to her gorgeous descriptions. Finally, she would state her price, and by no art or persuasion would she give way a penny afterwards.

I believe she was given to fits. Anyhow, she fell very ill once when she came and had to be given brandy to support her. I was afraid she was going to die in the house, which would have been exceedingly unpleasant, for it is a heinous breach of gentility to be found mixed up in any such transactions. We are so foolish, we have such little minds, we try to hide our doings from our neighbours, who are all going through the same experiences and are equally desirous of concealing them from us. If all our screens were taken away what a comedy of errors would be disclosed. How surprised we should be to see everyone committing follies of which we have been so ashamed and so anxious to hide from the eyes of all!

After all, the brandy had a most beneficial effect. I think it must have flown to her head, for never before had she given such large amounts. I was quite sorry to find her so well at her next advent. Her sniff was even more eloquent and her prices had returned to their original low level. I regret now that I did not again try the brandy.

Another woman I employed was even uglier than the first. She was so wholesomely ugly. A great red full moon represented her countenance, radiant with the colour of the Eiffel Tower. She was altogether a more satisfactory chancellor than the other. She always insisted on your stating your own price to begin with. 'Well, what d'yer think yerself, mum?' was her invariable ejaculation, and then, hearing your reply, she would break in on whatever you said by, 'It ain't worth more than *'arf* that to me, mum,' in the most aggrieved voice. I became used to her in time and, knowing she would halve whatever I said, used to demand double the worth of the thing. 'What d'yer think yerself, mum?' You grow so tired of your opinion being thus asked. I wonder how many times she says it in a day! It is a cautious way of going about it, at any rate. If that woman ever appeared in a police court on a charge of dishonesty and the magistrate asked her what she had to say to the charge, the answer would undoubtedly be, 'Well, what d'yer think yerself, sir?'

Some of those bills are still unpaid. Quarter day is coming round again, so I expect there will be some more soon. Alas! I am an unlucky being, born under an unlucky star.

You may think it a strange notion, but I attribute all my ill-luck to spiders:

If you wish to live and thrive,
Let a spider run alive.

I am not superstitious as a rule, but I cannot help thinking that my wholesale massacre of this obnoxious insect has something to do with my misfortunes by way of retribution.

I hate spiders! Nearly everybody has a pet aversion of some sort. I have heard people shriek at the sight of a caterpillar, and turn pale in the neighbourhood of a toad. My great antipathy is a spider! Not that I object to its treatment of flies – nasty little worries, they deserve everything that happens to them. But it is the *appearance* of a spider that is so against it. There is a shifty expression about the eye and such a leer on the upper lip. Money spinners are not so objectionable. I can tolerate them. It is the big, almost tarantulas, from which I flee. Those creatures which start up suddenly and run across the room close by where you are sitting; creatures so large that you can almost hear their footsteps as they pass.

A man told me once he had found a spider in his room of such enormous dimensions that he had to open the door in order that it might get out!

Overdrawn, you say? Well, it sounds a little improbable certainly; not so much on account of the unusual size of the spider as for the extraordinary consideration on the part of the man.

3
ON POLITICS

Perhaps you don't think me competent to talk about politics? 'What do women know about such things?' asks the superior masculine mind.

Well, they don't know so much as men, I admit, and I earnestly hope they never will. A woman who is infected with politics is a positive pest and should be removed at once. If I do not know anything about them, at any rate I ought to, as I have been brought up in a raging Tory household and so have been steeped in them from my youth up.

There is such a sameness in politicians. Whatever their opinions, their language and feelings are all one. They are only directed at different people. While one man is gloating over a Conservative victory you hear a mutter from the Radical to the effect that 'That *brute* has got in for —' Poor man, why, because he thinks differently to you, should he be a brute? But just the same words are spoken if the positions be reversed. It is only the mouths that change places.

I am afraid my views incline towards the Tory side. I cannot help it, I was bought over long ago. You *must* feel an interest as to the successful candidate when the result means either a tip all round or a thundery atmosphere for the rest of the day. Men take an adverse poll as a personal affront and vent their feelings on their families. The tipping was quite an understood thing when I was younger; now it is given up and joy is shown in a less substantial way, I regret to say. Unfortunately the thunderstorms are not events of the past as well.

Politicians have such a narrow way of looking at things. The other side can do nothing right while they themselves are absolutely faultless! If a Tory wishes to confer an opprobrious epithet on a person he calls him a Radical, and vice versa; the opposite faction is capable of any enormity! This reminds me of the old Scotchman who, on being asked his opinion of a man who had first murdered and then mutilated his victim, answered in a shocked voice, 'What do I think? Well, I think that a maun who'd do all that would whistle on the Sawbuths!'[7] 'Such a man must be a Home Ruler,'[8] my father would have said.

In having a guest with opposite views at your dinner table, what agonies do you not suffer? I have gone through those dreadful meals, trembling at every word that drops from the man's lips. Try as you may, turn the conversation how you will, there is sure to be some allusion, some statement, that sets on fire all the host's enthusiasm, and it does not take long before the poor guest is entirely annihilated and subdued – unless indeed he is as hot on his side as the other is on his; then indeed all we can do is to sit and hear it out. To attempt to stem such a torrent would be the act of a lunatic. We only feel thankful that 'pistols for two and coffee for one' is a thing of the past.

The general elections are dreadful times; nothing but canvassing goes on night after night for weeks beforehand. Conversation is entirely restricted to the coming event – if you mention a word about anything apart from it, you are considered absolutely profane and are treated as a pariah for the next few days.

It is interesting, I admit, and the election day itself is positively exciting. You cannot help catching the malady at times. I remember once, when I was very little, and walking out with my governess, tearing down a Liberal bill, in spite of all she said to the contrary. True, it was on what she considered her own side, though I don't think she knew enough to distinguish between the two; still, her real annoyance was occasioned more by the look of the thing. That a pupil of hers should act in such a plebeian way, and in so public a place, certainly must have been somewhat provoking. Anyhow, she gave me a bad mark for disobedience, which affected me but little, as when I related the story to my father later on he rewarded me with a shilling for my prowess! Electioneering, you see, is not good for the morals!

How tired you get, too, of seeing the names of would-be members stuck up all over the place. My brothers used to follow the Liberal bill-sticker round and, as soon as he had turned his back, pull the placards down, or cover them up with their own. This was found out at last, and the foe grew more cautious.

Then the extravagant promises made by the candidates, which they never really intend to fulfil, and could not if they wished. It is like the man in church who, while singing,

> 'Were the whole realm of nature mine,
> That were an offering far too small,'

was rubbing his finger along the rim of a threepenny bit to make sure it was not a fourpenny!

On election days all mankind goes mad. Their excitement is so great that they would scarcely know it did they forgo their dinner. And this, with men, proves an absorbing interest in the matter. Anything placed above dinner, in their opinion, must be important indeed.

There is such a polite element abroad on polling day. Men are so respectful and hurl such affectionate terms at one another. Even the dogs are upset and strut about in quite a different manner than on ordinary days, so puffed out with vanity are they, on account of their decorations. The members' wives and their friends are all taking part in the scene too, bringing voters along in their carriages and shaking hands with everybody indiscriminately. I heard an old navvy protesting once that 'Lady — never troubled to shake 'ands with him any other time, but was generally that 'orty she'd step over you as soon as look at you.'

Poor old men are dragged out *nolens volens*[9] to add their mite to the public voice and are sometimes so aged that they scarcely know what their opinions are. I hope I shall not live to be very old. It is a terrible thing when you make such a prolonged stay on this earth that you have to be helped off it.

It is very curious, too, how exceedingly disobliging old people are. I know a family who have never worn anything brighter than grey for years. 'In case we have to go into mourning soon – our poor old aunt, you know. It's so very sad!' and they squeeze a tear out from somewhere, but whether on account of their relative's illness or her prolonged life is open to opinion. The old lady is flourishing still and the family is as soberly clothed as ever. When she has been dead a few months what rainbows they will become, to make up for lost time!

'A disappointing man,' I have heard a dutiful nephew term his uncle. True, he (the uncle, I mean) is ninety-four and therefore old enough to know better than to rally so many times. But after all, he does nothing, runs into no danger, is tended as carefully as a new-born baby; I should not at all wonder if he still continued 'disappointing' and took a new lease of life for seven years. But I am digressing and must return to politics.

I went to a Primrose meeting[10] once and the experience was not so happy as to make me wish to try it again.

It amused me, certainly. The conclusion I eventually arrived at, when I left, was that the chief element in the Primrose League was gratitude! This virtue seemed to be the point round which all the speakers rallied.

First the secretary rose, ran off a quantity of statistics, as to what had been done by the great League, what it was going to do and how many converts had been induced to join, which was exceedingly uninteresting, I think, but which elicited loud applause from the rest of the audience. Then some resolution was passed, at which if you agreed you were begged 'to signify the same in the usual way'. After which, those who thought differently were asked to show their feelings in the same fashion. I held my hand up here, but I suppose the ruling councillor did not expect any opposition, for he never even looked round to see, but gabbled off by rote, 'On the contrary? Carried unanimously!' and my amiable attempt at running counter to the rest was not even noticed!

Then the ruling councillor gave way to Mr — (here a sickly smile was directed at the great man), who had so very kindly come to speak to us this evening, who would, he felt sure, quite enchant us with his – er – great eloquence (another leer to his right).

The great man then came forward and, with a superior smile on his countenance, waited until the applause which greeted his entrance had ceased and then began. He commenced somewhat softly, detailing all the advantages of the Primrose League: what it had done for England, the fear it arouses in the heart of the Liberal faction, how it will raise the country to a summit it never before has reached! No! and never would have reached had it not been for this flourishing, this powerful League! &c., &c., &c. His voice gradually grew louder and louder until, with beating his hands on the table, stamping violently over the sins of the Radicals and perspiring vehemently in the effort, he presented anything but a pleasing spectacle.

Of course animation like this brought down the house. The applause nearly deafened me and I was quite glad when he drew near the end of his most tedious speech. He concluded by calming down very suddenly, returned to his original tones and, thanking his audience for his exceedingly kind reception, retired to his seat looking, as Mr Mantalini would say, a 'dem'd damp, moist, unpleasant body'.[11]

Then up rose the ruling councillor and called us all to pass a vote of thanks to the 'gifted orator'. Someone seconded it, and the great man came forward again to thank us for thanking him. A sort of 'So glad, I'm glad, you're glad' business, it seemed to me.

Then the ladies were thanked for being present: 'Such great aids, and such an *important* element in the League', with a snigger, and what he confidently hoped was a fascinating smile, but which made him resemble a very placid cow with the corners of its mouth turned up. Such a mouth, too! The poor man could have whispered in his own ear had he wished. Then someone returned thanks for the ladies. The ruling councillor was thanked, and thanked his thankers back again, and after a few more people had exhibited their great faculty for gratitude the meeting broke up – the only moment at which I felt inclined to applaud.

I do not wish to disparage my own 'side' by the foregoing remarks, not caring in any way to emulate Balaam.[12] It is not only the members of the Primrose League who are so anxious to praise each other. It is the case at nearly every meeting you go to. It is a weakness of human nature. We know that if we laud our friend he will sing a eulogy on us the next minute, so it is only natural we should do it, after all.

The fault is not in our stars,
But in ourselves, that we are underlings.[13]

4

ON AFTERNOON TEA

The Muses' friend, Tea, does our fancy aid,
Repress the vapours which the head invade,
And keeps the palace of the soul serene.[14]

How I do love tea! I don't deny it, it is as necessary to me as smoking is to men.

I have heard a lady accused by her doctor of being a 'tea-drunkard'! 'Tea picks you up for a little time,' he said, 'and you feel a great deal better after you have had a cup. But it is a stimulant, the effect of which does not last very long, and all the while it is ruining your nerves and constitution. I dare say it is difficult to give up – the poor man finds the same with his spirits. You are no better than he!'

It is rather a come-down, is it not? Somehow, when you are drinking tea, you feel so very temperate. Well, at least, the above reflection makes you sympathise with the inebriates, if it does nothing else; and I am afraid it does nothing else with me. In spite of the warning, I continue to take my favourite beverage as strong and as frequently as ever, and so I suppose must look forward to a cranky nervous old age.

It is curious to notice how men are invading our precincts nowadays. They used to scoff at such a meal as afternoon tea, and now most of them take it as regularly as they stream out of the trains on Saturday afternoons with pink papers[15] under their arms – such elevating literature! Indeed there is quite a fuss if they have to go without it – the tea I mean, not the paper.

It is strange, too, because they dislike it so if we trespass on their preserves: e.g. their outcry on ladies smoking, which is exceedingly unfair, for we have no equivalent for the fragrant weed. Still, I agree with the men in a way, for nothing looks worse than a girl smoking in public, though a cigarette now and then with a brother does, I think, no harm, provided it does not grow into a habit.

My brother once gave me a cigarette and bet me a shilling that I would not smoke it through. It was so hard that, if I had bent it, it would have snapped in two. He had only just found it in a corner of a cupboard, where it had lain for years and years. But oh, the strength of that cigarette! It took me hours to get through, for it would not draw a bit. Nevertheless, with the incentive of a shilling to urge me on, I continued 'faint but pursuing' and eventually won the bet. I would not do it again for ten times the amount.

But I should be talking about tea, not smoking; and tea has other baneful influences besides destroying the digestion. I think that afternoon tea is the time that breeds more gossip and scandal than any other hour in the day.

As Young exclaims:

Tea! How I tremble at thy fatal stream!
As Lethe dreadful to the love of fame.
What devastations on thy bank are seen,
What shades of mighty names that once have been!
A hecatomb of characters supplies
Thy painted altars' daily sacrifice![16]

Acquaintances drop in. They have all the latest doings of the neighbourhood at their fingers' ends and in a quarter of an hour have picked every one of their most intimate friends to pieces, nor do they leave them a shred of character.

Why do we feel such a relish in running down our friends and relations – the latter especially? *I* quite enjoy it, though

I should never do so outside my own family; thus my words never come round to their ears. It is a necessity to relieve your feelings occasionally, and your family is a good, safe receptacle.

For those who have a taste for speaking spitefully of their neighbours, I can suggest an amusing game which was, I believe, started in Oxford. It is called Photograph Whist and is played by four. Two or three dozen photographs are dealt round and each person plays one, he who plays the ugliest portrait taking the trick. The more hideous the photograph, the greater its value as a trump! I have played the game with a man who always keeps his brother to the end and then brings him out with enormous success, the said brother never failing to overtrump any other card in the pack! So you see it is a most amiable game altogether. You must only be careful not to spread your doings abroad, or no one will present you with their portraits ever again.

There is no sin so bad as being found out. You can say anything as long as you are not discovered to be the originator. But if your words against a person ever happen to get round to him or her (of course, added to and made almost unrecognisable in their progress) you make an enemy for life. At least, this is so as a rule. Personally, I never care what people say against me, so long as it is not true. But if they only keep to the truth, then it is aggravating. You cannot deny it! You cannot 'tremble with indignation, and fling the words back in their faces', as the slandered heroine always does in the modern novel. You must simply submit to the accusation.

A man I know was saying all round the place a little while ago that my sisters and I 'were all good-looking until we opened our mouths'. Of course we heard of it, and have never forgiven him for his 'damning praise'. But it is true. We always admit the fact. We know we show our teeth too much when we laugh and talk. It was impossible to disclaim such a statement. If he had said that we squinted, not a syllable would have been pronounced against him. Our eyes are all exceptionally good and would bear any detrimental remarks. But no, he kept to the truth and consequently has suffered ever since, for ways of revenge have been found which were thoroughly successful. He is the ugliest man I ever met, too, and should therefore have been the last to offend.

In spite of the tea you are invariably given on such occasions, I think calls – formal calls – are some of the most dreadful experiences Mrs Grundy[17] obliges you to undergo. I dislike them immensely and always get out of them if possible. I hope servants do not afterwards record the expression of my countenance when they tell me their mistress is 'out'. It is radiant with an unholy joy!

These dreadful 'at home' days, too, are so provoking. If you know a dozen people in a neighbourhood, you can only call on one at a time. They all have different days! This may seem slightly impossible; but it is not indeed. While one lady's house is open to visitors on the first and third Wednesdays in the month, another is on view on the second and fourth, and so on. Not two people agree!

Small talk, I think, is never so small as on these occasions. The poor weather is thoroughly worn out, a few mutual friends are picked to pieces and, of course, there is a discussion about dress. Sometimes you hear some sad account of the lady's second cousin's daughter, and you have immediately to clothe your countenance in a sober garb. You must look grieved, and all the while not caring one straw if the cousin's daughter has fits or gets insane, or anything else she cares to do. You have never heard of her before and therefore have not the slightest interest in her eccentricities. I always feel so terribly inclined to laugh, just because I ought to be doing the other thing.

People are so fond of talking about their troubles and griefs. The greater the sorrow, the greater the discussion. They call up tears to their eyes, as if the subject were too sacred to approach. But such tears are kept for the purpose. They come at their bidding and fall as naturally into their place as if the exhibition had been practiced beforehand. It is a positive enjoyment to such people to detail their grievances.

With the lower classes, this, so to speak, gloating over your losses is even more apparent. One comparatively well-to-do woman I know seems to have a monopoly of funerals. There is always some relation dead, and off she goes with an important air, draped from head to foot in black: the picture of 'loathed melancholy' outwardly; inwardly, glowing with pride; while all her neighbours stand outside their doors, literally consumed with jealousy at her good fortune! And then the terrible moment of her return, when you are obliged, whether you will or not, to listen to the whole account, the description, the progress and finally the interment of 'the corpse'! I hope, however dead I may be one day, that I shall never be described as 'a corpse'! There is something so horrible in the word, I always think. It makes you even more dead than you are. It cuts you so absolutely off from the living.

Then there are those tiresome people who talk of nothing but their own families. The mother from whom you hear all the ailments of her children if they are young, all the conquests of her daughters if they are old. The sisters, to prevent the accusation of vanity, do not praise themselves, but arrive at the same end by lauding up each other! These 'mutual admiration' families, as Wilkie Collins so aptly terms them, are families to be shunned.[18]

You do not very often come across men on these 'at home' days. If they are in the house, they wisely avoid the drawing room; and if you ever do meet one, he is sure to be a very milk-and-water young man – one who delights in small talk and small matters; or else a curate.

I met one of the former class the other day. He was a dreadful specimen! A large head, a bland smile, a vacant stare and an enormous capacity for eating!

He came and sat by me when I first arrived; but when he made a slip of the tongue and I brought it to his notice kindly, but firmly, he went away and sulked for the rest of the afternoon.

He was talking about the recent muzzling order and added, in quick little tones, 'They are talking about muzzling cats, I see.'

'But cats do not bite,' I objected.

'No,' in mild surprise at my ignorance; 'but they scratch.'

'And do they intend to muzzle their paws?' I asked, smiling; adding a suggestion that two pairs of galoshes apiece would answer the purpose admirably, besides having the combined advantage of keeping the poor things from rheumatism!

But he did not smile. He saw nothing funny in what he had said. He thought I was laughing at him, and so left me at the very first opportunity, and went and sat by himself at the tea table. I could not very well see what he was doing, for his back was turned; howbeit it was a very eloquent back – a back which appeared absorbed in bread and butter and cakes! He must have cleared the table, I should think, before he had finished!

It certainly is not nice to be caught up suddenly and made to appear foolish. If you ever make a mistake, the best way is to confess it at once, to tell the tale yourself. It sounds very different from your lips than from those of your dearest friends. People laugh, but it is a laugh that lacks the sting it would have if someone else told it at your expense.

I remember making a woeful slip when I was taken over a cotton mill. The man who was conducting us pointed to what looked like a heap of dirty wool and explained that it was the raw material. 'And is that just as it comes off the sheep's back?' I asked unthinkingly. If a thunderbolt had fallen in our midst the guide could not have been more astonished. 'Cotton, Miss!' he said with grave surprise, '*cotton* is a plant!' I enquired for no further information in that cotton mill, but I told the story myself when I reached home, joining in the laughter that followed as heartily as any of my audience.

Curates are more the rule than the exception at the five o'clock meal. Somehow, you always connect the two. Afternoon tea without a curate sounds an anomaly, a something incomplete.

I have had great experience in curates. Ours is a large parish and many clerical helps are needed. Large, small, nice, objectionable, ugly, handsome – I have met specimens of each and all, and have come to the conclusion that the last kind is the worst. How rarely do you meet a good-looking man who thinks of anything but his appearance. It is strange, for the more lovely a woman is the less apparently conscious she is of her beauty. At any rate, she does not go about with an expression which seems to say, 'I am that which is "a joy for ever" – admire me!'

The 'pale young curate' type is perhaps the most general. This poor thing is so depressingly shy – I say depressingly, because his shyness affects his company. You try to draw him out. You ask question after question, and have to supply the answers yourself, only obtaining, by way of reward, despairing upward glances that are by no means an encouragement to proceed.

The most fatal effect of this shyness, however, lies in the fact that he dare not get up to go! He sits toying with his hat; he picks up his umbrella three or four times, and lets it drop again; finally, starting up with a rush in the middle of a conversation, he hurries out, shaking hands all round with everyone but his hostess!

Would it be a very heinous breach of etiquette if, after an hour and a half of this curate's company, one should suggest diffidently that it was time to go?

In strong contrast, there is the bold, dashing man who only comes when he knows all the daughters are at home, not so much because it gives him pleasure to see them, as because he would not deprive them of the pleasure of talking to him. He has a faith in himself that removes mountains; no lady's heart can beat regularly in his presence, according to his confident opinion.

So, on the whole, I do not think afternoon tea is so nice abroad as it is at home. It is not so pleasant with many as with a chosen few. I am selfish, I am afraid, but I must confess I enjoy mine most with the sole company of a roaring fire, a very easy chair and a novel!

5
ON DRESS

I do not know who was the originator of the remark, but it has often been said, and is generally admitted, that women do not dress to please the men but to outdo one another.

I think just the same might be said of men in their turn. It is after all this spirit of competition which helps to make the world go round. It is innate in man, and woman too, to always try to outrun each other.

With clothes it is undoubtedly the case. The ancient Briton must have vied with his neighbour in different designs with the woad plant. An unusual curve, an uncommon pattern, caused, I dare say, as much excitement then as the fashions of our own day.

I often wonder how they will manage some points in the histories for the coming generation. In most of these books you see illustrations and descriptions of the dress of the period, the costume of the reign. How, O historians, can you show forth those of Victorian times? Fifty years have passed already! There were four seasons in each of those fifty years! Two hundred illustrations must be shown in order to give a correct idea of the dress of the time! Perhaps it might be more satisfactory to devote a volume exclusively to the subject.

If only we did not run on so quickly! We seem to get faster every year. In a very little time, what we wear one day will be quite out of date the next! When we arrive at this climax, there will be a sudden convulsion of nature, I should think, and we shall return once more to the more simple garb of the aborigines. What an amount of trouble it would save us! No worrying because the dressmaker has not sent our gowns home in time! No sending them back to be altered! No dressmaker's or tailor's bills; or at the least, very small ones, for 'woad' could not ruin us *very* much.

So, on the whole, it would be well perhaps if this revolution did occur. Some such convulsion as geologists declare has already frequently befallen our earth; and, as they prophesy, is shortly coming again.

I do not like talking to these scientific men. They make you feel so infinitesimally small. They go back such a long, long way. They make out that from the creation (which by the way they do not admit, only considering it another great change in the world springing from natural causes), from the creation until now, is the space of a moment on the great clock of time, is a mere 'parenthesis in eternity'.

It is not nice to feel such a nonentity. What are our lives, our little lives in comparison? We, who each consider ourselves the one person upon the earth, the hero or heroine in the great drama, all the rest mere by-characters; we do not care to be considered of such little consequence, only puppets appearing on the stage for one moment and taken off the next. We are ike the clergyman in the small island off the north of Scotland who prayed for the inhabitants 'of Great Cumbray and Little Cumbray and the neighbouring islands of Great Britain and Ireland!' On our small piece of land, we yet consider ourselves the centre of the universe.

It is to be hoped if this revolution occurs, after all, that the climate will change likewise. We should require something more besides blue paint in most of our English winters!

Perhaps we take too much thought for what we shall put on. They say that nothing but the prevailing and forthcoming fashions fill the feminine mind. It is true sometimes, I dare say, and yet I always agree with our immortal bard in thinking that 'Self-love is not so vile a thing as self-neglect.'[19]

34

It is decidedly better to think too much than too little. It is a duty to your country and your nation to look your best, no matter who is likely to see you.

Of course it can be overdone: e.g. the lady who insisted on her bonnet being trimmed on the right because that was the side presented to the congregation! And she, I am afraid, is only a type of many.

There is no reason why this should be the rule; yet nearly everyone seems to bring out their new clothes on Sunday and exhibit them in church. I suppose it is because they meet so many friends there and with laudable unselfishness wish them all equally to enjoy the sight.

'What's the good of your going to church?' a man said to me once. 'You only go to show off your gown and look about to see who has a new bonnet and who has not! Now, when *I* go,' he went on in a superior way, 'I don't notice a single thing anyone has on!'

'No,' I answered quietly, 'but you could tell me exactly how many pretty girls were among the congregation, and describe their features accurately!' And he not only forbore to deny the accusation, but admitted it with pride! No girl, he assured me, with any pretence to good looks, ever escaped *his* notice.

Which was the worse, I wonder; he or I? At least I did not glory in my misdeeds.

'*Il faut souffrir pour être belle*', and I *have* suffered sometimes. How often I used to burn myself when I first began to curl my hair! This is such an arduous task, too, with me, for my hair is, as my old nurse used to call it, 'like a yard o' pump water' (I never went to her when I wanted a compliment). It certainly is straight, and I find it a matter of great difficulty to give it the appearance of natural curls. But 'practice makes perfect', they say, so I still persevere, hoping that it may come right some day. I have to be so careful in damp and rainy weather. It is such a shock to look at yourself after a day's outing, to find your 'fringe' hanging in straight lines all down your forehead, an arrangement that is so particularly unbecoming. You begin to wonder at what time during the day it commenced to unbend and if you have had that melancholy, damp appearance many hours. Perhaps it is as well that you did not know before, for it could not have been rectified; you cannot bring a pair of tongs and a spirit-lamp out of your pocket and begin operations in public! Still, it is exceedingly aggravating if you think you have been making an impression and you return home to confront such a dejected-looking spectacle as you find in your mirror.

I am wandering again. Let me get back to my subject – dress. To ensure a good fit you must have your gown so tight that it is impossible to raise your arms. You are obliged to walk about stiffly, with all the appearance of a trussed fowl. If you wish to put on your hat you must first unbutton your bodice! It is particularly awkward, too, in church: you scarcely have the power to hold your book at seeing distance. But what do such trifles matter? You look as if you had been melted and poured into your gown. What are a few discomforts, more or less, when you have procured an effect such as that?

I always like to look as tall as possible. Five feet four is not a very great height; so, to give the appearance of another inch, I have my skirts made as long as possible: that is to say, they just don't sweep the pavement, and that is all. But, oh, the trouble of that extra inch! Unfortunately I have no carriage, my present pecuniary condition does not permit me the luxury of hansoms, and I always avoid an omnibus, where you have fat old men sitting nearly on the top of you, wet umbrellas streaming on to your boots, squalling babies and disputes with the conductor continuing most of the way – not to speak of the time you have to wait while so many roll by 'full inside'! So on muddy days, when I take my walks, the amount of distress I have to undergo on account of the length of my gown is inconceivable. I grow weary with holding it up and have to stop in the middle of the street to change hands, and when you have an umbrella as well, and sometimes a small parcel besides, this performance is anything but a momentary matter. You drop your gown, the umbrella changes hands and the parcel generally falls in the mud! While picking it up, four impatient, wet, mackintoshed pedestrians knock against you, and go off uttering imprecations on your head. And when you are once again comfortably settled, your satisfaction does not last long. Your left hand tires as soon as your right and the scene has all to be acted over again.

There is a great deal of '*savoir faire*' in holding up. Your gown must be high enough to quite clear the ground, but then comes the danger of holding it too high. There has been no licence yet granted for the exhibition of ankles in the great metropolis either by Mrs Grundy or the county councils; therefore 'holding up' becomes a very delicate performance.

Though we do not dress only to please the men, I always prefer their criticisms on a costume to those of my own sex. You can never tell if the latter speak the truth. They may be jealous and run it down from spite; they may want to gain something from you and so call yours 'a perfection of a gown, and suits you admirably, my dear!', disliking it exceedingly in their inmost hearts.

But a man never gives his approbation unless he really means what he says, and he is not difficult to please as a rule. So long as the costume is neat and well fitting, he does not care about anything else. It is the *tout ensemble* he thinks of, not the thousand and one details that go to make up the whole.

I wonder why so many men dislike large hats! It is a pity, for they are so very becoming to some faces, and give a picturesque effect altogether. Perhaps this last is a reason for their disapproval. They never like their womankind to attract attention.

The most unpardonable sin one woman can commit against another is to copy her clothes and bring the style out as her own idea. It is intensely irritating! If she admits she has copied or asks your leave beforehand, it is a different matter. You are even gratified then, for 'imitation is the sincerest flattery'. But to have your ideas stolen and brought out in such a way as to convey the impression that you are the imitator to say the least arouses murderous intentions in your heart!

There are times, too, when you receive a shock to your vanity; times when you are quite satisfied with your appearance and find to your dismay that everyone is not of the same opinion.

I remember once when I was dining out and feeling very pleased with my *tout ensemble*, I was disillusioned in a way that upset not only my self-confidence but my gravity at the same time. To heighten the general effect, I had stuck a patch near my mouth. (Oh, the minds of the last century! From whose fertile brain did it emanate, I wonder, the fact that a piece of black plaster on the face should be so eminently becoming!) Imagine my horror when the maid, an old servant I knew very well, took me aside and whispered confidentially, 'Oh, Miss! You've got *such* a big smut on your chin!'

Clothes are altogether a great nuisance, I think. How tired you get of the regular routine of the morning toilet; always the same, never any variety. Why are we not born, like dogs, with nice cosy rugs all over us, so that we should just have to get out of bed in the morning, shake ourselves and be ready at once to go down to breakfast and do the business of the day?

'Ah well! God knows what's best for us all,' as an old charwoman said to me, years ago, when she was remarking on how I had grown. I never saw the application of the remark and do not think I ever shall. Whether my growth was a subject to deplore, and she tried to comfort me, or not, I cannot say; but she was evidently proud of the remark, for she repeated it three times!

6
ON CHRISTMAS

It is such a prickly time. Not only everything but everybody is positively bristling with prickles. Go where you will, you cannot avoid these pointed, jagged edges. You come across them everywhere and have to suffer accordingly.

To begin with, there is the holly. Now you could not find anything lovelier in the way of foliage than holly, only such a little suffices. At Christmas time you are literally saturated with it. In every house you enter, in everything you eat, at every step you take, nothing but holly, holly, holly.

Then there are the church decorations, begun generally a week beforehand. All the ladies of the place assemble in the vestry, attracted there by diverse reasons. Some by the desire to have a finger in every pie; some because it is an opportunity to meet the curates; and some, but a very few, from real love of the work. I cannot understand these latter, I must confess. It is the most disagreeable work I have ever undertaken. Such dirty work, too! Your hands or your gloves grow perfectly black under the operation; and it is a curious thing that when this stage is reached, your nose invariably begins to itch, and you forget the condition of your fingers, and – well, the result is anything but becoming! It is so comfortable, too, walking about the vestry, isn't it? The holly grows so affectionate to your ankles, and at every step squash goes a berry, and all its middle oozes out and sticks to the sole of your boot. When you go home, you find you are at least an inch taller by reason of the many corpses of berries you have collected!

Yes, Christmas decorations are delightful altogether. And so the clergymen think when they become excited in their sermons and bring their fists down sharply on some charming arrangement of holly round the pulpit. They do not actually swear then, but their faces express sufficiently all they would like to say; it rather spoils the effect of the discourse, especially if the text be on the virtue of patience.

As I said before, everybody is prickly at Christmas time, especially one's relations. And so, to make the season as festive as possible, we, in our sensible way, collect as many of these cheerful, sociable beings together as we can; and, in short, make a delightful family party. Holly? It is an insult to the tree to compare it in any way. No, I think the whole gathering resembles a hedgehog more than anything else. It is one *mass* of prickles. Ah, these happy family parties! Is there ever one member that agrees with another, I wonder?

There is the crabbed old maiden aunt, always on the defensive, never without the idea that someone is waging war against her. Yet she has to be treated civilly and humoured. Has she not that which some people term 'filthy lucre' but never really think so? Have these old ladies ever had any youth? Have they ever danced and enjoyed themselves like other people? What has made them so sour, so bitter? Is it disappointment or regret? Poor old souls! In spite of their money, they never seem happy. They are to be pitied, I think, though they do try to make themselves as disagreeable as possible. They are so independent, too, they will not be interfered with. They know everything better than anyone else. One old lady I used to know declined altogether to have a lawyer, insisting on making her will herself. It was found afterwards, fortunately not too late, that she had appointed herself her own executor!

Then there is the maternal grandmother, to whom, of course, the host is openly rude. This wears you out more than anything, for you have always to be ready to smooth over and soften every sentence that is said. And she never helps you at all either. If she can possibly put her foot in it and unconsciously irritate her son-in-law more than ever, she does it.

Then the uncle who spends his life in making the most villainous puns you ever heard. Not a remark, not a word in any assembly, which this witty specimen of humanity does not at once garnish with a pun of the poorest description. It generally has to be repeated twice, too, for it is never noticed the first time. The poor pun, indeed, has a most melancholy existence, for it is greeted with no other applause than that emanating from the author of its being, and stirs up a torrent of abuse from the maiden aunt, who thinks the laughter is directed at her.

Why were punsters ever invented, or family parties either? They are our thorns in the flesh, I suppose, and so must be endured.

After dancing attendance upon these lively old people during the day, the least you expect is a good night's rest to support and invigorate you for the battles on the following day. But no, at Christmas time any repose is denied you.

You are just off to sleep, forgetful of all troubles and strife, when you are rudely awakened and brought back to the present by the most awful screechings under your window. Morpheus flies. He has a musical ear has that god, and when once, 'Oh, come let us adore him' – with a concertina accompaniment, both voices and instrument woefully out of tune – when once these harmonious strains have started, that good old deity goes, to return no more that night.

Where does the pleasure come in, I wonder? Certainly not to us fuming inside; and surely not to those poor deluded people squalling outside! It must be so cold, so raw; and they never get appreciated, these so-called 'waits' – oh, if they only would *not* wait, but go away somewhere else, how much more satisfactory for us all!

No, Christmas is not a soothing time. It does not altogether improve your temper. How glad I am when the festive season draws to a close and the last petitioner for Christmas boxes goes on his way rejoicing. To me it always realises that period so often referred to by the lower classes, 'a month o' Sundays'. So much church and so few posts!

It certainly is a little more interesting when the presents come in. There is a kind of excitement about them; and it is not until the following day, when you find yourself with a dozen letters of gratitude to indite, that you feel that perhaps, after all, you might have done without them.

There is nothing so annoying as being obliged to write letters when you do not feel inclined. It is a great art, this letter writing, and very few possess it. People often think they do, and they write for writing's sake; but these letters are most wearying to read. Between every line you seem to see the words, 'Is not this a charming letter?' and in reality you are so bored it is all you can do to reach the end. Then those dreadful persons who 'cross and recross' their epistles in every direction! Paper is not so dear but that they could at least afford a flyleaf. They defeat their own ends, too, for their letters are never legible, and they have to write again to explain their meaning, thus paying another penny away in postage.

Why do we not make a stand against the old forms? Why should we always tread in the footmarks of our ancestors, instead of making tracks of our own? 'Dear Mr So-and-So,' we write to a man almost a stranger to us. Imagine his surprise if we addressed him so to his face! And we end in just such a foolish and unreasonable way, 'Yours obediently, faithfully, truly!' Where is the sense? Your signature should be quite enough. You have to be so careful, too, in saying whether you are obedient, faithful or affectionate to your correspondent. If you end too warmly, by mistake, the whole letter has to be written again. It is not a thing you can scratch out or correct. It would look so very bad.

People have different ideas of 'Christmasing'. Some prefer to adopt an unsteady gait and to spend the night in a ditch or a police station; some have a taste for family parties; some like it better by themselves: and some go right away and spend the time at a different place every year. These last are, I think, by far the most sensible. It is a mistake to have landmarks to remind you how time is running on, how friends have left, how the loved ones have passed away. The vacant place appears even more empty. The old happy times show out even happier in contrast to the present. You cannot enjoy yourself or forget the past, for

A sorrow's crown of sorrow is remembering happier things.[20]

It is far better to go away somewhere to places which recall no sorrows or recollections and have no associations with the years gone by.

He is growing such a foolish old man is Father Christmas. He rarely visits us now with hoary head, his garments sparkling with frost and snow. He is tired of all that. He likes a change of fashion, like everybody else. He either comes so thickly enveloped in yellow fog that you can scarcely distinguish the old man, or else he arrives so drenched with rain and splashed up to the beard in mud that we scarcely like to open our doors to him.

He is growing old, I suppose, and trembling on the brink of second childhood, so we must not blame him. But still he is not a very great favourite of mine and I cannot refrain from echoing the complaint in one of the comic papers – '*Why doesn't he strike, like the rest?*'

7
ON THE COUNTRY

At which season, I wonder, is the country most lovely, most enjoyable! Is it in the spring, with its richly coloured carpet, its young green leaves, its delicious perfumes, its glorious freshness? Ah, why cannot we, like the trees, put off our old sinful world-steeped habits and, year by year, bud out in purest innocence once again? The hedges, but a week ago barren and bare, are now clothed in brightest apparel, the greenest of cloaks thrown over them, lifting up their heads and sharing in the general rejoicing, in the glory of their annual resurrection. Is it in summer, with its myriad blooms, and its thousand thousand happy voices, the silent torpid river, basking in the light of the sun, and responding only to the fishes as they frisk near the surface? Or is it in the autumn, with its many shades, with its long avenues on which nature has lavished whole tubes of burnt sienna and vermilion; when you tread on gorgeous paths heavy with golden leaves? Oh, why are we not as lovely in our autumn of life as nature is in hers? Why, when she decks herself in the gayest colouring, do we don our soberest garb? *We* do not gain in splendour as we grow older. We lose our beauties and our charms one by one, till at last we stand destitute. O cruel Time to treat us so!

> *Time that doth transfix the flourish set on youth,*
> *And delves the parallels in Beauty's brow.*[21]

And yet 'God tempers the wind to the shorn lamb.' While He takes from us our youth, He also takes away the inclination to be young. We pine for the happy days of childhood; yet, if the power were given us, who would wish himself back in the past? We feel we should always like to be young, but should we not get very weary of the world, should we not wish for some kind of change?

Or is nature at her best when the year is dead and the earth puts on her spotless white shroud, when everything around has fallen asleep and only robins are left to join in the wake?

Unanswerable question. There are too many opinions. Some prefer winter, some summer; some like the heat, some like the cold. Only in one thing do we agree, and that is in our taste for variety, for change. Much as we admire the country, lovely as it is, it would not suit many to live there all the year round. The peace and quiet of our woodland scenes make us enjoy the town life all the more, while the unceasing turmoil of the season makes us hail with delight the idea of once more being

Far from the madding crowd.[22]

The very thought refreshes you. There is something exhilarating in our journey country-wards, long and tiring though it may be. Few people care about a railway journey and yet, with one or two kindred spirits, I think it most enjoyable.

Travelling alone in the midst of strangers, you do feel rather melancholy. You try to read, and when you are tired of chasing the words up and down the page, you look out of the window and admire the scenery as you flit past until your eyes ache to such an extent you are obliged to withdraw your gaze and be satisfied with the study of human nature, as far as it can be procured from the inmates of your compartment. Finally you go to sleep, only to wake up after a few minutes, to find the eyes of all your fellow passengers upon you, and this serves to make you nervous and uncomfortable. You dare not close your eyes again. You feel sure it is the signal for everyone to turn in your direction and you will not gratify them.

Then comes luncheon time, when we all begin to grow fidgety, and take surreptitious looks at our watches, and then glance round at our companions to see if anyone is taking the first plunge. Hopeless quest! Nobody ever *will* be the first to begin to eat in a railway carriage. Why is it, I wonder? Are they afraid none of the others will follow suit and they be left to eat all alone? It would be nervous work, certainly. You would feel so dreadfully greedy, and yet if you offered any of your fellow travellers even a sandwich, they would peek up their heads, give you an astonished look and decline shortly but with decision. You are made to feel you have insulted them, and yet they had such a hungry expression! Rarely indeed, though, do you undergo such an experience. You only have to rise and reach down your basket, and behold! the next moment all the carriage is feeding. We are nothing but sheep after all. One leads the way and we all follow.

When you have once made a start, eating on a railway journey is easy enough work; it is when you grow thirsty that the difficulty comes in. You pour the sherry, claret, whatever you have (some take milk in a green bottle – not a very tempting beverage to look at!) on to the floor, over your gown, on your neighbour's foot (thereby eliciting a most unholy frown from the recipient of your bounty), anywhere, indeed, except in your glass. Even if you are fortunate enough to catch a few drops, it is another Herculean effort to take it to your mouth. No, drinking in the train, while it is in motion, requires years of practice.

Then again your fellow passengers are not always all that can be desired. Often they are neither pleasant in themselves nor interesting as a study. I travelled with an awful old lady the other day. She had six small packages with her in the carriage, besides her handbag and umbrellas and half the contents of an extra luggage van. The long-suffering porter who had looked after her boxes and finally put her in the train was crimson with his exertions. The generous lady, having searched several pockets before finding the necessary coin, bestowed on him a threepenny piece for his trouble! 'Thank yer, mum,' he went off muttering grimly, 'I'll bore a 'ole in the middle and 'ang it round my neck.'

This good dame never ceased to worry all through the journey. She pulled her things from under the seat and put them up in the rack, and then reversed their locality. At each station she called frantically to the guard to know where she was and if she ought to change. Finally, when we reached our destination, it was proved that she had taken her ticket to one place and had her luggage labelled to another; and there she was, standing on the platform gesticulating violently, while the train was steaming off with her belongings. What happened I do not know, for I was hurried off by my friends; but I should think it would be long before she and her luggage met again.

Fortunately she never knew how near she was to her death. If ever I had murderous intentions in my heart, it was on that journey north.

You do not feel very affectionate towards the country on a wet day. Indeed, it is a most mournful affair altogether, unless you have a particularly merry house party. There is absolutely nothing to do. The heavens weep at such inopportune moments, too. There is sure to be some large picnic, some delightful gathering on the '*tapis*', when they choose to exhibit their griefs. And they never notice how unwelcome such a display of feelings is, but go on weeping,

weeping, weeping all day long, until at last you catch the malady yourself, and are obliged perforce to mingle a few of your own tears with theirs.

No, there is simply nothing to be done, and Satan has quite a difficulty to find enough work for all the idle hands. Some can be perfectly happy spending all their time in solving the intricacies of those many wonderful puzzles which have appeared lately as a sort of antidote to the mischief generally supposed to be perpetrated by the aforesaid gentleman. Unfortunately an entirely contrary effect is produced on me. They did not look far enough ahead when they made me. They could not conceive the wonderful minds of this time and so did not endow me with a sufficient quantity of patience. If they could have imagined those marvellous little tin saucers, with shot running in and out of horseshoes &c., with *me* in the perspective, well, I think they would have gone about their work more carefully, and perhaps brought about a happier result. As it is, the puzzles are always swept away now at my approach. I have smashed so many.

It is base ingratitude, too, on my part, to bring them to so speedy an end; for what I owe to those dear little things I am powerless to express. Those entertaining people who sit speechless and only answer yes and no with an eternal smile on their faces: give them a puzzle. There is no further effort to amuse them required on your part. They are at once absorbed in 'shot'. Their only idea is to successfully get them into their places. They never do; but, being good thorough-going characters, will never give up the attempt.

You meet several of these people in the country, but they never get very friendly. You shock them too much with your 'London manners'. They vote you 'fast', and turn aside, fearful of contamination for their daughters.

Oh, the dreariness, the heaviness of a country dinner party! It seems to last four times as long as any other – parish, horses or crops the only topic of conversation. How can you be interested in old Jane Smith's rheumatism when you have never heard of her before; in the swelling of a favourite mare's hock when you did not know it possessed such a thing? People's views grow so dreadfully narrow, shut up in their small parish. Their stock of conversation is so very small. It is wise to find out your dinner partner at once and avoid that man as you would a disease until the meal is announced. If not, if you accidentally get in his neighbourhood and he talks to you, all his conversation is at once exhausted and you are obliged to hear it over again at table, or submit to an interesting silence.

Dinner parties anywhere are, I think, a mistake. It is a wicked waste of time to spend nearly three hours over eating and drinking. And you require such a very interesting 'taker-in' to make it bearable at all.

The river is the nicest way of spending a holiday, in my opinion; you are so free and untrammelled. Mrs Grundy even waives some of her laws on the river. The smaller the cottage, the more primitive the place, the more enjoyable it is. You can spend your time on the water, and when you are tired of that, you can hire a pony and trap and drive through some of the loveliest bits of English scenery, to your heart's content.

Only be careful before engaging your pony to find out its previous occupations. It is a necessary caution, I assure you. It once took me nearly an hour to drive out of one of the smallest villages imaginable. And why? Because my pony had formerly belonged to the butcher and insisted on first going his rounds! I coaxed, I persuaded, I lashed him, but it was all of no avail. On he trotted until he reached the familiar doors of his late customers, and then he stopped and *would* not go on for at least five minutes. One place was worse than any. I could not get him away for over a quarter of an hour. This rather mystified me until I was told later that the butcher was on 'walking-out' terms with the cook residing there!

8
ON TOWN

There is not much difference of opinion as to when town is at its best. Perhaps a few misanthropists, wrapped up in their little selves and their narrow thoughts, would shut themselves up during the season, in order to escape the pain of witnessing us all in our ungodly career. Shallow butterflies they call us. And what do they know about our lives? They judge from appearances; and because we wear a cheerful expression, shutting down our cares and struggles in our inmost hearts, and not burdening other people with them, we are called shallow and worldly. No, you good and godly people, what do you know about us? You are no more capable of judging than the ephemera, which lives but for a day and so must consider the world all sunshine, all light. How can it imagine the night which closes round later on, when neither it nor any of its ancestors has ever lived to see it?

You ought to be punished for your ignorant mutterings. You complain of the well-dressed happy throng. You should be turned out in the streets in August and September, and if the utter destitution does not shortly turn your brains back in the right direction I am afraid your case is hopeless.

Does any place come up to London, I wonder? Having never been out of England I cannot give an opinion. Unfortunately I have not the gift, like some people, of either imagining or describing places I have never seen – descriptions generally gleaned from other books and com-piled under one authorship as original compositions. Why cannot they be content with laying their English stories in English scenery: places they know well and can write about? Some save up their money in order to go abroad and visit one particular place, so as to bring new scenes into their new books. But ah, how weary you get of this one place! It is brought into at least three of their next novels. Everything, past, present and future, seems to happen there. Your one prayer, as you lay down the book, is to the effect that they may soon be able to save up a little more and visit another spot.

There is so much going on in May, June and July that it is a difficulty to get through all your engagements and yet see everything there is to be seen. Then there is the Park. Two or three hours of the day must at least be spent in the Park. There we all come out to show ourselves and to look at others. There the equestrians canter up and down the Row. Such equestrians too! If foreigners take their ideas of English riding from the Row, they must form a high opinion of our horsemanship.[23]

There are the loungers flocking around their friends or walking up and down in the hope of admiration. And they get it, too, for who could help admiring such masterpieces of a tailor's skill? Are these really the descendants of that Adam whose posterity had all to earn their bread by the sweat of their brow? These automatons, whose only business in life seems to be to look after pretty women and themselves? Men are supposed to be breadwinners, but they have a very easy time of it, I think, though they generally try to make themselves out so overworked. Go into that great centre of business, the City, and you find every one of these busy men out and about, always apparently in a great hurry, never seeming to arrive at any destination, running about and hustling each other, occasionally meeting an acquaintance, which proves a good opportunity for one to stand the other a 'drink'. A funny way men have of showing their affection, have they not? 'Ah! How de do, old fellow? Come and have a drink,' is their invariable salutation to an intimate friend. After all, it is better than the mutual kissing on the part of women, which is the more emphatic the more they dislike one another. Men are less demonstrative and therefore more sincere in their friendships. Anyhow, there cannot be many at work in their offices, or where could this idle crowd come from?

In spite of their haste, though, they generally find time to stare at any woman who crosses their path. Why should not a woman go to the City? She has as much right there as man, and yet if she is in the least degree superior to the flower girls who surround the Royal Exchange, she is looked on as a freak of nature, a positive curiosity, and is followed by every pair of male eyes within reach!

Mrs Grundy is inclined to rather overdo her season, I think. There is so much she might leave undone, so many things that 'never would be missed'. Imagine the gratitude that would be displayed to anyone who would put down and demolish those dreadful crushes, so-called 'at homes', where nobody ever is at home; where you have neither space nor air from the moment you arrive until the glad time comes for departing. Does anyone enjoy them, I wonder? Does anybody like being literally baked with heat, which I am sure must exceed even that at Mexico, where one of the inhabitants of that delightful climate, when he died and went to perdition, found the contrast so striking that he was obliged to send home for his greatcoat!

Still, I suppose such entertainments will continue to exist. They are a good deal cheaper than balls or dinners, and you can 'knock off' ever so many people at the same time.

It is well, at any rate, to consider economy in some matters in these woefully extravagant days. When the shops are decked out in their gayest colours to lure us on to destruction, why is it that 'just the very thing you want' is placed so conspicuously in the front of the window, put cunningly near a mirror, too, so that you see it all the way round and it appears doubly precious?

How convenient it is, by the way, when they have mirrors in the shop windows. You can look to see if your hat is straight, or your veil nicely arranged, without being credited with vanity. You are supposed to be admiring the bonnets displayed to view, not yourself. Girls make a great mistake when they take little surreptitious glances at any mirror they come across. The action is always noticed and condemned; while if they, instead, went up boldly, ostensibly to smooth their hair or alter a pin, it would be taken as a matter of course.

It so soon grows into a habit, this always looking about for your reflection, and one that is very difficult to get out of. Not that the men are at all behind us in this respect. There are not many of our little follies that the lords of creation do not take up and cultivate. You see them at dinner, addressing nearly all their conversation opposite – where hangs a mirror. At dances they are admiring and smiling at their reflections the whole evening, finding far more satisfaction in gazing there than at their partner, even though she be the loveliest in the land.

But to return to my subject. (I seem to be always wandering away.) You need never be idle in town. A wet day even makes no difference when a place teems with picture galleries, as London does. They are such good places to meet your friends. You always see someone you know. You might as well be there as anywhere else. Of course you do not look at the pictures. You glance at the few you have heard talked about, just so as to say you have seen them. But you do not go to a picture gallery to look at *pictures*! 'We always go the wrong way round. You avoid the crowd like that, you know,' I have heard people say. '*Avoid* the crowd!' It is the crowd they want to see! There is less chance of missing your friends if you go in the opposite direction! There is one real advantage, though, in beginning at the other end. You don't have the same people following you all the time, nor have to listen to ignorant remarks. 'Who's that? She don't look very happy, to be sure,' I once heard one woman ask of another as they were going round. 'That? Why, that's Adam and Eve, o' course, and the serpent in the distance. I never 'eard of anyone else who went about without their clothes on, though why they put chains on her I can't think: it says nothing about 'em in the Bible.'

I glanced at the picture. It was 'Andromeda'![24] And they talk of the strides education has been making of late years!

9

ON CHILDREN AND DOGS

Are you very shocked that I should couple these two subjects? An insult to the children, do you say? Well, do you know, I am afraid I consider it an insult to the dogs. I am not fond of children and I love dogs. A man may be a superior animal to a dog, but a puppy is decidedly more intelligent than a baby. What can you find more helpless, more utterly incapable, than a baby? Look at a puppy in comparison. At a month old it is trotting about and growing quite independent; more sensible altogether than a child aged a year.

I am afraid I shock people often by my opinions, but they are really genuine. I am always more interested in the canine race than in the blossoms of humanity. Very likely it is the behaviour of each that makes me so. Children never take to me, nor come near me if they can help it. I do not understand them or know what to talk to them about. On the other hand, dogs will come to me at once and, what is more, keep to me. I have never been growled at in my life and I have come across a good many dogs, too.

'You were a baby yourself once!' How often has this been said to me when I have aired the above opinions. It is put before me as an unanswerable argument, a sort of annihilating finale to the conversation. Yet I really don't see what it has to do with the matter. I suppose I was a baby once. At least they say so. Which protestation, by the way, rather leaves it open to doubt, for '*on dits*' like weather forecasts are nice reliable institutions if you do but follow the opposite of what they tell you. Still, as there is more than one witness to the effect, I will give in and admit it: I was a baby.

But the admission makes me no fonder of the species. If anything it makes me admire them the less; for if I at all resembled the photographs that were taken of me – 'before my eyes were open', I was going to say; at any rate before I could stand – I wonder a stone was not put round my neck and they did not drown me in the first bucket of water they came across.

It is said that ugly babies grow up the best-looking and vice versa. This is a pleasant and comforting thought for the ugly baby. It can bear a little depreciation now, because it can look forward to the time when it will far outdo its successful rival. And the pretty baby's glory is soon over. It becomes only a memory which rather irritates than soothes. For after all, retrospection is not so pleasant as anticipation.

The above remark was said before a child about four years old the other day. She must have been listening intently and, having taken in the sense, she inwardly digested it, for the next time she quarrelled with her sister she broke in spitefully, 'You must have been the beautifullest baby that ever was born.'

Children should never be seen until they are over two. Until then they are neither pretty nor entertaining. But at this age they begin to say funny things and so are interesting. 'You only care for them when they amuse you!' cried a young mother once, indignant at my selfishness. I suppose it is a selfish way of looking at it, but if modern children were brought up as we were brought up I should not object to them in the least. We were always kept strictly in the nursery, only appearing downstairs on the rarest occasions; and when we arrived there we behaved properly – we were seen and not heard. We did not run noisily up and down the room, taking up the whole conversation of the party. We did not try to make the most disagreeable personal remarks; or if we did we were sent upstairs at once, and not laughed at for our 'sharpness'.

There are no children nowadays; they are mimic men and women. They dine late, they stay up until the small hours and are altogether as objectionable a faction as can be. They respect their father and mother not a whit. It was only two or three days ago I heard a child of five allude to her father as 'the fat old governor' and simply get laughed at for her remark, no one joining more heartily than the said parent himself. Of course, with such applause, the child repeats it again and again.

They have such dreadfully sharp eyes, too, these children. Not a defect escapes their notice. You tremble to hear what will come out next. They ask Mr Jones what makes his nose so red. They want to know why Mrs Smith puts flour on her face. In spite of a thick veil, they discover at once that Miss Blank has a moustache and enquire of her with interest if she is a man!

There are some nice children, of course – there are exceptions to every rule – and if they are pretty I cannot help admiring them. It is fortunate that I have never had anything to do with children. If I were a governess I should be so dreadfully unjust; I should always favour the pretty ones. I love beauty in any form. There are girls I could sit and look at all day, if they would let me. Only they are most of them so self-conscious; they expect to be admired, and when I see girls laying themselves out for admiration, however beautiful they may be, however strong my inclination to gaze, I will not gratify their vanity. For it is certainly true that though we prefer the praise of men, we do not disdain any like offering from our own sex.

That is the best of very young children. They do not notice you, they are not yet awake to the power of their charms, so that you are able to look your full. I say 'very' young, because it is a knowledge that comes to them only too soon, and a little of this knowledge is, at any rate, 'a dangerous thing'.

Children sometimes set you thinking more than any philosopher who ever existed. Their ideas are so fresh, so unsophisticated, so original. The atmosphere of the great unknown still seems to cling to their souls. They are not yet tainted with the world's impure air. They ask you questions impossible to answer, but which you are obliged to parry in an underhand manner, so as not to expose your ignorance. They solve problems and reach conclusions after a way of their own which, at any rate, have plenty of reason about them. I remember being very much struck by a little boy's idea once when his mother was remarking on the strange appearance of a man who, while his whiskers were black as ebony, possessed hair of a snowy white. 'But why, Mother, should it seem funny?' broke in the child. 'Aren't his whiskers twenty years younger than his hair?'

Dogs certainly cannot talk or say quaint things, but they can do nearly everything else. At any rate, they can understand you and distinguish between the words, as the following instance proves.

We have family prayers at home and have had them ever since we were quite little things. What an ordeal they used to be, too! We used to be watched so strictly, and the moment our eyes wavered from our books, attention would at once be drawn to the culprits, covering them with confusion. Woe be to him, too, who forgot to turn over the leaf of his book with the rest! It is such an unkind thing to do to print all the books alike. If you forget and turn over later, you are at once detected. Being sharp children, however, we used to make this our first care, so that whatever we were doing – laughing, pinching, winking – our pages all went over together, so we *sounded* attentive.

Our little dog was even more cunning than ourselves. He was never permitted, on any plea, to lie before the fire. 'It enlarged his liver,' his master said. Now this decree is a great deprivation to dogs. They like warmth and comfort just as much as we do; indeed, they love the fire to such an extent that if all the terrors of Hades were put before them, they would by no means have a salutary effect. The dogs would try to be as naughty as possible in the hopes of getting there.

But this particular little animal was made of most obstinate materials and had no intention of being balked; so directly we knelt down for prayers, he scrambled from under the table and stretched his full length before the fire. He knew he would not be spoken to until we had finished and felt quite safe until we all joined in the Lord's Prayer at the end, when he would immediately decamp and thus escape any scolding for his disobedience. It was more especially clever of him because we all joined in the Confession as well, but he never took any notice of that and always put off his departure until the last minute.

We had this dog twelve years altogether, and a sad night it was, indeed, when he had a fit and died. The breakfast table next morning presented a most distressing spectacle. We were all positively swimming in tears. The whole family was upset at his death; and when, later on in the day, he was wrapped up in a fish basket and buried in the garden, next door to a favourite rabbit – on whose grave a cabbage had been planted, most unkindly reminding him of the sweets of life he had left behind – we all lifted up our voices and wept again.

I often wonder if we shall meet our faithful dumb friends hereafter! Sages say no; but I cannot believe they are so entirely blotted out, and like to think they have some happy sugary existence somewhere, and that we shall see them again some day.

Dogs are very human, after all; they have a great many of our virtues and nearly all our vices. I expect it is this that endears them to us, for 'One touch of nature makes all the world kin.' They are just as contradictory, as disappointing, as ourselves. Why will they always show off to such bad advantage? After spending weeks in teaching them and fortunes on pieces of sugar, why, before an audience, will they insist on ringing the bell when they are told to shut the door; and when you ask them to sit up and beg, *why* do they die for the Queen?

A little while ago we used to have grand steeplechases with our dogs. We put up fences and water jumps, all of which – with the aid of sugar again – they were able to master in time. I think they used to get quite excited themselves at last. Our old gardener, who used to watch the races with great interest, told me once that he ''ad seen one of the little dawgs a'jumpin' backwards and forwards over that 'ere bit of wood [the highest and most perilous jump], and a'practisin' by hisself!' He *was* a very clever 'little dawg', but I don't think he ever reached such a pitch of intelligence as to practise 'by hisself'.

We had to fill up the fences down to the ground, or, to save themselves the trouble of getting over, they would run under or scramble through in some extraordinary fashion, which in the end took much the most time and pains. Humanity again! Lazy people always take the most trouble!

When I was a little girl I had every morning to learn and repeat to my governess three verses from a French Bible. I thought I had hit upon an easy way of getting over this and of reducing the quantity I had to commit to memory; so I chose the 136th Psalm, in which you will find, if you care to look it up (I have just had to do the same to find out the number, not being by any means a living concordance to the Psalms!), that half of each verse is composed of the words 'for His mercy endureth for ever'. Ingenuity wasted! Trouble increased! Not one whit the better off was I. Until that Psalm was finished I had to learn six verses instead of three. I retired anything but satisfied and heartily wishing I had left that Psalm alone. It was very mean of my governess all the same. She should better have appreciated the craftiness of her pupil. But, poor things, they have to be very sharp and always on the lookout, or the children will take them in; they will not let any opportunity escape them, and, indeed, I pity anyone who has the care of these unravelled Sphinxes, these uncut Gordian knots.

10
ON CONCERTS

I am not thinking about the Albert Hall concerts, where the highest in the musical world go time after time, always singing the same songs.

Neither am I thinking of 'Monday Pops'[25] and purely classical concerts, to which at least half the audience listens with closed eyes and thoughts somewhere in dreamland. They like to be thought musical; they know they ought to appreciate *such* renderings of *such* compositions; and, after all, when they describe 'the treat they had! Such a perfect touch, my dear, and the execution!' no one knows they have never heard a note, so what does their inattention matter? They have been seen there and that is all they care about.

No, my thoughts take a much lower range. They are intent on only amateur productions, from penny readings upwards, to those superintended by the elite of the neighbourhood, when the seats rise in price to five shillings each.

They are such nice cheery entertainments, so much life, such a great deal of energy, about them! You are called on by four separate people to take tickets. In desperation you have to yield at last, paying extra for having your seat reserved, or else you must start half an hour beforehand and scramble in with the crowd. There is generally a series of them, too, and you are obliged to go to them all. They are so considerate, these concert-makers, they would not allow you to miss one for worlds.

There is a great deal of novelty and variety about the artists themselves. All the musical members in the neighbourhood are routed out and each is persuaded to contribute to the public pleasure – by the way, there is never very much persuasion needed. It is such a treat to listen to people you know and whom you have heard perform dozens and dozens of times before in every drawing room in the place. At least you know what to expect. You recognise each song, each piece. You wait in suspense until Miss Brown has passed her high A – always half a tone too flat. You take it as a matter of course that Mr Black – the first violinist in the place – after tuning up for ten minutes, will break a string directly he begins to play. I should have thought he would be pretty well used to it by now, but he never gets in tune again for the rest of the evening. You would be quite disappointed if Mrs Green ever concluded her most finished and spirited pianoforte solo on the right chord.

These concerts always begin with a pianoforte solo and the performers ought to feel very flattered at the way in which they are received. We, the audience, regard them no more than we do the mounted policemen in the Lord Mayor's Show. They are not part of the procession. They are only meant to clear the way and let us know that the concert is going to begin, and then we must leave off our chatter. Naturally, we make the most of our time and try to get all our talking done at once. In fact, we are so taken up with what we are saying that we actually forget to applaud when the performance is over.

After the introduction in this form, the chief moving spirit of the entertainment comes forward and, after bowing right and left, stammers out (the chief moving spirit is never a good speaker) that he much regrets that, on account of Mr Jones, Mr Smith and Miss Blank having been prevented by illness from turning up, he is afraid there will be a little change in the programme. Now, as Mr Jones, Mr Smith and Miss Blank are down for seven things between them, there is likely to be a very great change in the programme. Why is it that people never know they cannot come until the last moment, I wonder? Perhaps they think that the more often they disappoint the more they emulate the 'stars' in the musical world. Only the force of example, you see. And, after all, what does it matter? The other performers are most kind and sympathetic, and ready to help all they can. They are delighted to sing four times each instead of twice. Selfish people! They have no consideration for the audience, they only think of their own enjoyment!

There is the youth who looks as if he were going to favour us with a sweet treble. Lo and behold! He opens his mouth and out comes a loud double-bass voice that seems to spring somewhere from the region of his boots. It is not a pretty sound by any means.

There is the smiling, simpering girl who comes forward gorgeously arrayed in light blue satin. She chooses a song, all trills and little scales, running up and down, shaking at last upon a high note for nearly two minutes and then coming down with a rush. This brings down the house. We applaud lustily; we begin the encoring business here, which, having once started, we do not intend to give up again. We like to get as much as we can for our money, we Britons. She keeps us waiting some time, too – taking a little refreshment in between, perhaps – and then comes back beaming with smiles and, under the impression that she is a second Patti,[26] shrieks out in plaintive tones, 'Home, sweet home!' A cat might as well try to emulate a thrush! And we never find it 'sweet' either. Never do you dislike 'Home' more than when you hear it sung thus.

There is the sentimental man who gets into position while the introduction to his song is being played. He sticks his finger down his collar (the object of which I can never understand), pulls both cuffs out, stretches out his music a yard or two in front of him and gazes above the audience with a hungry, yearning look. His is always a love song, an unhappy love song, that should bring tears to our eyes, only we are so taken up with his expression, and the fear that he is going to die or have a fit, that we have no time for weeping. True to our instincts, he is greeted with deafening applause, and, coming back, he generously treats us to the last verse over again.

Everyone is not so fortunate in receiving an encore, though. It depends on how well they are known, not on their deserts. The newcomer in the neighbourhood tries her hardest and does her best, but as we have never seen her before we scarcely take the trouble to applaud her, which must be rather disappointing, especially when her mother is sitting among the audience with the encore song on her lap, ready to hand it up.

The best exhibition of all is made by the flautist. He is the only one who plays that instrument for miles round and so the swagger with which he steps on to the platform is perhaps excusable.

How anyone *can* play it I do not know. It is such a singularly unbecoming instrument. But the wretched owner never seems to think so. When he once commences he gives us a good dose of it. We begin to think he is going on all night. Suddenly there comes a pause and applause is started at once, we being only too delighted to make a little noise on our own account. But no – it is a mistake, a delusion, after all. The pause was only an interval between an andante and a scherzo; and, with a bland smile at his ovation, on he goes again for another quarter of an hour. We – the audience – are disappointed, we feel we have been tricked, and we therefore sulk for a season. But the scherzo is so long, it gives us time to get over our ill-humour, though we are mutually resolved that we will not have him back again. Vain hope! From the far end of the room comes thundering applause, which never dies away until the talented flautist appears on the platform again. We find out afterwards that he treats the whole of his establishment to the cheap seats; so, of course, poor things, we cannot blame them. They are only earning their wages. Perhaps they are presented with an extra shilling each when their master returns home.

It is a curious thing how we all like applauding and making a noise. If you notice, at organ recitals in the church we feel quite uncomfortable. We think we ought to do something at the conclusion of the pieces; so, as we may not clap our hands, we all give a little rustle and cough. This is to show our approbation. *Every*one coughs. It is astonishing how many people have bad colds. For my part I think it is a pity applause is not allowed. It is infinitely preferable to the coughing at any rate.

Of course the comic singer goes down best. He is called back three, sometimes four times. The schoolboys behind grow excited and greet him with a whistle that would do credit to the 'gods'. This is too much for decently clad minds, anything so profane as that whistle. The clergyman, who is in the chair (the proceeds are always to be devoted to some charitable object), rises and insists that 'If that most objectionable noise does not cease, the boys will have to be turned out.'

Where the 'objectionable' comes in I cannot think. The boys are very clever to be able to do it. I have often tried it and cannot succeed, and so conclude it must be a difficult accomplishment. They stick about four fingers in their mouths and thereby make quite a different sound to any ordinary whistle. However, it is no wonder the chairman discourages it. When he was reading a few minutes before, reading out some dry little tale with a moral, in which the humorous parts were the heaviest, no encore whistle was accorded him. He was clapped loudly, of course – is he not one of the chief men in the parish? But no one wished to hear him read again, so we stopped our applause just in time to prevent him from reappearing.

We go home glad at heart, and two mornings later read an account of the evening's performance in the local paper.

We find there a few statements which agree with our own feelings. They say that 'Mr Jones sang in a pure and cultured manner, and deserves special attention for his sweet tenor voice and the refinement of the sentiment in his songs' (whatever that may mean!); 'Mr Smith played two violin solos with remarkable precision of touch and with the greatest ease'; while 'Miss Blank, with a good contralto, was all that could be desired in both her songs!' They were none of them there, but that does not matter. They were praised up more than anyone else, which must be very discouraging to those who *did* perform. But on account of their non-appearance alone we feel they deserve some approbation and so do not grudge it them. It is of no consequence to a newspaper reporter who is there and who is not. He takes the programme, ticks off the names and writes his remarks and criticisms just as he likes. It would be wiser, all the same, on his part, if he found out the absentees, for otherwise his little hints rather lose their effect.

He writes that this one wants a little 'animation', that one 'sings out of tune'. Miss So-and-So plays the piano 'with faultless manipulation, the only drawback being a slight preponderance of pedal', and so on. He generally has as good an ear for music as a parish priest who only knew two tunes: one of which was 'God Save the Queen' and the other wasn't. And once, when a brass band was playing a selection outside the vicarage, he went on to his balcony, hat in hand, and waved it vigorously as he commenced to sing the first line of 'God Save the Queen'.

Well, it does not matter after all. The only object is to appear learned and to use long words. If the artists do not like being ignorantly criticised they must forbear to appear in public, a result which would incline us to go and shake hands with the reporters all round in the exuberance of our gratitude.

11
ON DANCING

I was looking through a 'Querist Album' the other day; one of those dreadful confession books in which you are required to answer the most absurd questions. Dreadful indeed they are to write in, but not altogether uninteresting to peruse, though the interest comes not so much in the answers themselves as in the manner in which they are written.

Some go in for it seriously and describe their inmost feelings on the pages; some take a witty strain and put down the most ridiculous things they can think of; while others write just what comes first.

Some are such hypocrites, too. Here is a man who describes his wife as his ideal woman; and when we know that he scarcely ever addresses a civil word to the poor little woman, his admission is, to say the least of it, amusing.

'Have you ever been in love? and if so, how often?' This is one of the questions. The answers to it are of doubtful veracity. All the single ladies reply, 'Never!' underlining the word three times. 'Yes, only once,' is the statement of the married ones. According to the Querist Album, 'The course of true love *always* runs smooth.' No one seems to be attacked by Cupid but they must immediately marry the object of their choice, and 'all goes merrily as a marriage bell'. The men, on the contrary, like to appear somewhat inflammable. It is generally the masculine writers who adopt the sprightly key. Twenty – forty – thousands of times they admit falling in love. Such one-sided affairs they must have been, too; for the girls, according to their own confessions, never reciprocated any attachment until their rightful lords and masters appeared on the scene. I am afraid we must be a very hard-hearted race!

But it is the question relating to your idea of 'the greatest earthly happiness' that struck me most. 'Never being called in the morning,' was one lazy person's reply. 'To write M.P. after my name,' was the ambition of another. 'Married life,' wrote the bride on the completion of her honeymoon. Ah, little bride, you have been married some years now. Are your ideas still the same, I wonder? 'A good partner, a good floor, and good music,' said a fourth, and it is this one that has my entire sympathy. I agree with her. It is my idea also of 'the greatest earthly happiness'. I do not require much, you see. These are not very difficult things to procure nowadays; and yet I am often taunted with my love of dancing. If I express disapproval of a man, 'I suppose he can't dance,' they say with a sneer.

Now, though that accomplishment is a necessity in a ballroom, I do *not* consider it indispensable in a husband. Unfortunately you cannot dance through life. I wish you could for many reasons. A continual change of partners, for instance, would it not be refreshing? You would scarcely have time to grow tired of them. And how much more polite our husbands would be if they thought we were only fleeting joys! What am I saying? I am shocking everyone, I am afraid; the little matron who advocates married life, the newly made brides whose ideal men are realised in their husbands – I am shocking them all! I humbly plead forgiveness. You see, I am not married myself. I can only give my impressions as a looker-on, and, as Thackeray says, 'One is bound to speak the truth as far as one knows it, and a deal of disagreeable matter must come out in the course of such an undertaking.'[27]

But dancing *is* indispensable in a ballroom. If a man cannot dance he should stay away and not make an object of himself. Unfortunately, so many think they excel in the art when they have not the least idea of it. Again, with girls, dancing (in a ballroom only, of course) comes before charm of manner, before wit, even before beauty. I know girls, absolutely plain, with not a word to say for themselves, who dance every dance, while the walls of the room are lined with pretty faces, and dismal-looking enough they are too, which is very foolish of them. They should have too much pride to show their discomfiture.

Men have so much the best of it at dances – so everybody says. I am afraid I do not agree. I would not change our positions for anything. After all, a girl can nearly always dance with anyone she likes, and pick and choose as well as the men – provided, of course, that she is an adept on the 'light fantastic toe' herself.

And think, on the other hand, what men go through! Reverse the order of things, as you are supposed to do at leap year dances – which system, however, is never properly carried out. But suppose you go up to a man and ask him for a dance, and he tells you with a smile that 'he is very sorry, but really he has not one left'. Suppose that the next minute you see him give three to another girl, would you speak to that man ever again? *Never!* And yet this is what they constantly endure and, what is more, forgive.

After all, if you analyse it, what an absurd thing dancing is. Close your ears to the music and look around you when a ball is at its height. What motive, you foolishly wonder, could induce all these people – who are supposed to possess an average amount of brains – to assemble together to clasp each other round the waist, twirl round and round up and down the room, suddenly stop and hurry one after another outside the dancing hall, seeking dark corners, secret retreats, anywhere away from the eyes of other men? 'Ah, what a mad world it is, my masters!'[28]

How our grandmothers exclaim at the present mode of dancing – they who used to consider round dances almost improper! How the programmes must astonish them, too; those engagement cards that did not exist fifty years ago, and in their infancy were quite content to bear only two or three names on their paper countenances. But now times have changed and, as they grow older, they become most greedy little cards. They are not only not content with being scribbled all over, but require two names on the top of one another, and thus causing dissensions to ensue.

There is a great deal of art in making up a programme. It is a mistake to be full up before you arrive. Someone may come whom you did not expect and then you have no dance to give him. Arrangement of a programme requires two or three seasons' practice. There are the duty dances to be got through first; put them up early, so that they shall be soon over, and then you have the good ones at the end to look forward to.

Everyone has duty dances. There are your father's constituents, clients, patients, someone you are obliged to ingratiate, and these are generally the worst dancers in the room! One is so fat he shakes the hall as he walks, and yet is just as eager to join the giddy throng and, alas, to take you with him! Another resembles the little tin soldiers which schoolboys have such an affection for, in that he has been gifted with large flat stands, twice the length of himself, instead of feet. And oh, *how* he kicks! Then there is the complimentary man, a creature who never opens his mouth without making or implying a compliment. Does he ever find anyone whom this system pleases, I wonder! The only antidote I can find is to take no notice and pretend not to understand that the pretty speeches are directed at you. This discourages him after a time.

It is amusing to get hold of a man's programme and find out how you are represented there. They do not put down names, but describe costumes, hoping thus to find their partners more easily, but in reality plunging themselves into most hopeless perplexities. They scribble down 'pearl necklace', and find later that there are at least sixteen in the room, and so are worse off than if they had written the name.

Some describe the personal appearance, but this is a very risky thing to do. A man the other day wrote down his partner as 'Miss blue dress, with the nose', and subsequently dropped his programme, which, of course, was picked up by the lady mentioned. Now, I do not know why you should dislike being told that you have a nose – you would feel very much worse without one – but when your nasal organ takes up double its share of room in your face and is, moreover, prettily tinted with scarlet, which you try to conceal under a little pearl powder, and only succeed in making it purple – well, perhaps you would not like to be told you have a nose. At any rate, this lady did not, and hers very much resembled this description, I believe. But she was a wise woman. Not a word did she say on the subject, and he went home happily unconscious of her fatal discovery, until a few days later he received his programme back as a Christmas card, with 'Miss blue dress with the nose's compliments'. How very comfortable he must have felt when he met her next!

What a great many different styles of dancing there are! You have to change your step with nearly every partner. The girl should always suit hers to the man's, he has quite enough to do with the steering. You require about five good partners altogether and can then spend an enjoyable evening. A different man for every dance is tiring. You never get beyond the theatres and the weather; you have not time to say much more, and grow quite weary of the same style of conversation. I always think I must be a most uninteresting partner when I am asked what theatres I have been to lately, or what is my opinion of the Academy &c., &c. I never begin this kind of talk myself except as a last resource, when I can get nothing else out of a man. Someone says, I forget who, that 'a woman can always know in what opinion she is held by the conversation addressed to her', and is it not true? The foolish compliments paid to the pretty but silly little debutante; the small talk to the fools; the sparring with the witty; the risqué tales enjoyed by those of a more rapid style. Men find out first what are our tastes, and then dish up their conversation accordingly, and they do not often make mistakes.

Some girls dance with one man the whole evening. How weary they must get of each other! Engaged people invariably pass the evening together, and sometimes do not dance at all, but sit out in some secluded corner. They have to endure one another for years to come; I wonder they do not get as much variety as possible now. At any rate, they might just as well stop at home.

Like everything else, dancing is hurrying along and growing faster every year. The *deux-temps*, they say, is coming back. May the day be far ahead when that step reigns once more! Perhaps before then I shall be converted into a chaperone and shall sit watching others dance, not being able to do so myself; or, perhaps worse, not being *asked* myself. I am afraid I should not make a nice chaperone. I should look very cross and should hurry away as early as possible. Ah, sad indeed will the day be when I give up dancing, when only the remembrance of my past enjoyments will be brought back to me through the scent of gardenias and tuberoses, dear dissipated-smelling flowers!

12
ON WATERING PLACES

What a great deal of trouble and time it takes to choose a watering place! And yet there are many and various kinds of resorts, some for one season, some for another.

If you could be carried sufficiently high above the earth so as to have a bird's-eye view of the whole of Great Britain, what a strange sight it would present during the months of August and September! The county would appear surrounded with a human fringe, the outer edge more resembling a disturbed ants' hill than anything else. I don't suppose we should appear more significant than ants at that distance.

There are those places teeming with shopkeepers and children where you can scarcely see the beach, so covered is it with those who are making the most of their one holiday in the year.

There is the primitive little village, discovered by few, which is welcomed by the city man who wants rest and entire seclusion from business matters and the world for a month or two. And oh, what language he uses, and how annoyed he is to find absolutely nothing to do – one post a day and, worst of all, no newspaper until late in the afternoon! And this is the man who wishes to be shut out from the world and from his acquaintances! There is no pier; there are no amusements. The esplanade is composed of nothing more than a plank of wood, on which in walking you have to observe much caution in order to keep your balance; and sometimes the butcher from the neighbouring village forgets to call! In desperation, the unfortunate creature digs sandcastles with his children and, after a few days of his banishment, grows quite excited as the waves wash up and undermine their foundations. He picks acquaintance with anybody he comes across, be he peer or peasant – anything to make the time pass a little quicker until he can return to the stir of his business life again.

Someone remarks somewhere that 'A man works one-half of his life in order that he may rest the other.' I wonder if those who are successful ever appreciate their rest when they get it! I wonder if it comes up to their expectations! If the goal towards which they have been looking almost since they began to exist is worth the trouble and energy spent on it! Ah, I am afraid they very rarely find it so! They have become so immured in their busy lives that it is difficult to grow accustomed to any other. Unless one is brought up to it, the *Dolce far niente*[29] is not an existence we enjoy. We are made the wrong way about somehow. We ought to be born old and gradually grow younger as the years roll on. Still, I dare say there would be something to complain of even then, and perhaps it would not be very dignified to go off the stage as a baby!

To go to the opposite extreme, there are the fashionable water-places: little Londons, or rather little imitations of London; for beside that great capital itself they are like pieces of glass to a diamond. And yet fashion and folly are all here, sunning themselves by the sea instead of in the park; driving up and down in the same way, in equally charming toilets. But still there seems to be something lacking, something wanting. They are too small, these towns; you so soon know everyone by sight, and grow tired both of them and their costumes. There is a good deal of stir and life about all the same. There are bands, niggers,[30] clairvoyants, fire-eaters: plenty indeed for you to see and hear when you are weary of strutting up and down and nodding to your friends. And yet, in spite of all, you grow tired of 'London by the sea' after a few weeks, even in that dead season of the year – November.

Have you ever visited one of these places in the midst of a tennis week, when the grand tournaments take place? Lawn tennis is a delightful recreation for a time, provided you have a good partner and good antagonists, and you are playing under a moderately warm sun; but when you hear, see and play nothing else for a week, when the conversation is 'tennis', when no one appears without a racquet in his hand, when all you have to listen to are criticisms on the courts and balls, grumblings against the handicapping, imprecations on 'bisques' – well, you begin to hate the very name and wish you could injure the man who invented it. You grow tired of watching the same thing day after day, the men who spend their lives in tossing balls across to each other, the sea of faces turning backwards and forwards at each stroke with the regulation of a pendulum.

Yes, it takes a long time to decide on a watering place, and when at last you do make up your mind you have to change it again very soon because you find all your 'sisters, cousins, and aunts' have chosen the same resort; and really you have quite enough of your relations in town without their following you wherever you go. You require a little variety when you go away. An old lady I used to know always kept it a profound secret where she intended spending her summer holiday, 'Otherwise, my dear,' she said, 'I should have the whole family at my heels!' A most disagreeable old lady she was; and I know for a fact that her relatives always avoided her when possible (she was not blessed with very great possessions!), so that her caution was quite unnecessary. Oh, vanity of vanities, how little we know of the world's true opinion of us!

When you have fixed on your locality, there is even a greater difficulty to go through. You have to choose your residence; and this takes up even more thought and time.

There are the lodging houses, monotonous in their similarity. The same gilt-edged mirrors protected from the dust by green perforated paper; the same jar of wax flowers, standing on a mat which is composed of floral designs in Berlin wool – designs to which you can give any name you like – 'You pays your money and you takes your choice.' They represent anything, the whole concern hiding its modest head under a glass case; the same shavings in the grate, with long trails of roses gently slumbering on the top; yes, and the same voluble landlady, the whole of whose private concerns you are in possession of five minutes after you have taken the apartments.

There is the boarding house, advertised as 'Directly facing the sea'; and when you have engaged your rooms, and arrive with all your luggage, you find the establishment is at the far end of a side street; and 'Directly facing the sea' is interpreted by the fact that by hanging halfway out of the sitting-room window and screwing your head round violently to the left, you can see the place where that watery monarch ought to be.

'A boarding house is so much nicer than a hotel, because you get to know the people so much easier,' I heard a girl remark once. This is my chief objection to a boarding house. Because you are staying under the same roof, all the inhabitants consider they have a right to address you, and, what is more, they will not be repulsed, which, as most of them by no means move in the best society, is not at all palatable. The women you can tolerate, but the men are not to be endured. You are always coming across them, too. On whatever drive, excursion or trip you take you invariably meet 'boarding houseites', who are only too ready to recognise you. You can never get away from them; there is only the public drawing room, and there they come in and out, talking to you, interrupting you or else causing your ears to ache by their attempts at music.

The meals are somewhat amusing, as you can watch all your fellow boarders without being disturbed. They cannot talk and eat at the same time and so philosophically devote all their energies to their dinner.

There is the girl who scrapes up acquaintances with everybody. She has had the good luck to be placed near a man, and the demure way in which she prattles and smiles at him convinces you that she is trying to make the best use of her time. Sometimes he is absent and then the smiles give way to the gloomiest expression. Finally, on the arrival of newcomers, when there is a sort of general post all round, she is placed at the furthest extreme to her late partner, and oh! the wistful little glances she passes up the table to the gourmand who, oblivious to all but his dinner, scarcely notices her departure.

There are the three old maids, intent on capturing a husband. They have come here as a last resource. But with the usual fickleness of fortune, they seem to be more shunned by the male sex than attracted to it.

There is the newly married couple, looking very conscious and silly, as if they were the only people in the world who had ever committed matrimony.

There is one old lady grumbling, and objecting to the back of a chicken. Poor birds, they have only two wings each, and really cannot provide everybody with them! There is another furious, because on asking for a favourite dish that is down in the menu is told that 'it is all served!' The best things always are, unless you manage to get into the good graces of the waiter or waitress.

Young men and maidens, old men and children, all here, offering plenty of material for students of human nature!

Hotel life is very different. Even if you find the *parvenu* and *nouveau riche* as equally objectionable as the boarding-house species, at least they do not force their acquaintance upon you. The *table d'hôte* is much more entertaining and you are altogether more independent. Characters you come across occasionally that are most interesting to study. There are the girls who are taken the round of hotels by their mothers, in the hopes of getting them 'off'. There are the men who astonish everybody by their generosity and apparent display of riches, and finally decamp without paying their bill.

A man was telling me the other day of a certain 'black sheep' who had run into difficulty; how his family, after a great deal of trouble, managed to raise £200 between them and sent him off to America with the money to start afresh in a new country. In a month's time he was back again, penniless as ever, and cursing his luck and bad fortune. It was only by accident they discovered the bills of the best hotels in New York in his pocket, and found that he had been living like a prince while his £200 lasted, nor had tried at all to obtain any occupation.

With such consummate cheek, a man ought to get on in the world, I think, for, after all, it is self-confidence and 'bluffing' that seem to succeed most. However down in the world you are, however bad your 'hand', you only have to 'bluff' a little to make it all right. There are many foolish people in the world ready to be your dupes and luckily they never think of asking to 'see' you. Even the best of us try it on a little; we strive to hide our skeletons under the cloak of cheerfulness, and entirely disguise our real feelings –

Alas, our frailty is the cause, not we;
For, such as we are made of, such we be.[31]

NOTES

1. Lord Byron, *Don Juan*, Canto I, stanza 194.

2. 'Let us return to our subject'.

3. The mystery is that if Adam and Eve were created by God and Cain was their child, who did he find to marry?

4. Alfred, Lord Tennyson, *Maud*.

5. One of the four days in the year when payments became due. In England at the time this would have been Lady Day (25th March), Midsummer Day (24th June), Michaelmas Day (29th September) and Christmas Day (25th December).

6. Abbreviations for pounds, shillings and pence.

7. Sabbath.

8. A supporter of Home Rule for Ireland: in other words, a Liberal rather than a Conservative.

9. 'Whether willing or unwilling'.

10. The Primrose League was founded in 1883 with the aim of spreading Conservative values.

11. Mr Mantalini is a character in Charles Dickens' *Nicholas Nickleby*.

12. The Book of Numbers in the Old Testament tells the story of how Balaam is riding his ass when it suddenly stops. Though he beats the ass, it will not move. It then turns out that an angel has been standing in his path that only the ass can see.

13. Shakespeare, *Julius Caesar*, Act I, scene ii.

14. Edmund Waller, 'On Tea'.

15. The Saturday evening newspaper that printed the sports results used pink paper.

16. Edward Young, *Satire VI: On Women*.

17. Mrs Grundy, a character in Thomas Morton's play *Speed the Plough*, is the personification of conventional propriety.

18. 'A family in a state of mutual admiration' is a description used by Wilkie Collins in his book *Poor Miss Finch*.

19. Shakespeare, *Henry V*, Act II, scene iv.

20. Alfred, Lord Tennyson, *Locksley Hall*.

21. Shakespeare, Sonnet 60.

22. Thomas Gray, *Elegy Written in a Country Church-Yard*.

23. The 'Park' is Hyde Park and the 'Row' is Rotten Row, where people still ride on horseback today.

24. The painting of *Perseus and Andromeda* after Guido Reni in the National Gallery shows Andromeda chained to the rock.

25. The first of the Chappell Brothers' Popular Concerts were held in 1859 at St James's Hall in London. The 2,200-seat venue sold 1,000 tickets for a shilling and the varied programmes always opened and closed with major chamber works. The 'Monday Pops' were held in the evening and the 'Saturday Pops' in the afternoon.

26. Adelina Patti (1843–1919) was the highest-paid singer of her day.

27. From Thackeray's *Vanity Fair*.

28. From the title of Thomas Middleton's Jacobean comedy *A Mad World, My Masters*.

29. 'It's sweet doing nothing'.
30. This word was colloquial in England at the time. It had not yet become synonymous with racist abuse, though clearly in its usage it could be derogatory.
31. Shakespeare, *Twelfth Night*, Act II, scene ii.

HESPERUS PRESS CLASSICS

Hesperus Press, as suggested by the Latin motto, is committed to bringing near what is far – far both in space and time. Works written by the greatest authors, and unjustly neglected or simply little known in the English-speaking world, are made accessible through new translations and a completely fresh editorial approach. Through these classic works, the reader is introduced to the greatest writers from all times and all cultures.

For more information on Hesperus Press, please visit our website: **www.hesperuspress.com**

ET REMOTISSIMA PROPE

SELECTED TITLES FROM HESPERUS PRESS

Author	Title	Foreword writer
Pietro Aretino	*The School of Whoredom*	Paul Bailey
Pietro Aretino	*The Secret Life of Nuns*	
Jane Austen	*Lesley Castle*	Zoë Heller
Jane Austen	*Love and Friendship*	Fay Weldon
Honoré de Balzac	*Colonel Chabert*	A.N. Wilson
Charles Baudelaire	*On Wine and Hashish*	Margaret Drabble
Giovanni Boccaccio	*Life of Dante*	A.N. Wilson
Charlotte Brontë	*The Spell*	
Emily Brontë	*Poems of Solitude*	Helen Dunmore
Mikhail Bulgakov	*Fatal Eggs*	Doris Lessing
Mikhail Bulgakov	*The Heart of a Dog*	A.S. Byatt
Giacomo Casanova	*The Duel*	Tim Parks
Miguel de Cervantes	*The Dialogue of the Dogs*	Ben Okri
Geoffrey Chaucer	*The Parliament of Birds*	
Anton Chekhov	*The Story of a Nobody*	Louis de Bernières
Anton Chekhov	*Three Years*	William Fiennes
Wilkie Collins	*The Frozen Deep*	
Joseph Conrad	*Heart of Darkness*	A.N. Wilson
Joseph Conrad	*The Return*	Colm Tóibín
Gabriele D'Annunzio	*The Book of the Virgins*	Tim Parks
Dante Alighieri	*The Divine Comedy: Inferno*	
Dante Alighieri	*New Life*	Louis de Bernières
Daniel Defoe	*The King of Pirates*	Peter Ackroyd
Marquis de Sade	*Incest*	Janet Street-Porter
Charles Dickens	*The Haunted House*	Peter Ackroyd
Charles Dickens	*A House to Let*	
Fyodor Dostoevsky	*The Double*	Jeremy Dyson
Fyodor Dostoevsky	*Poor People*	Charlotte Hobson
Alexandre Dumas	*One Thousand and One Ghosts*	

Francis Petrarch	*My Secret Book*	Germaine Greer
Luigi Pirandello	*Loveless Love*	
Edgar Allan Poe	*Eureka*	Sir Patrick Moore
Alexander Pope	*The Rape of the Lock and A Key to the Lock*	Peter Ackroyd
Antoine-François Prévost	*Manon Lescaut*	Germaine Greer
Marcel Proust	*Pleasures and Days*	A.N. Wilson
Alexander Pushkin	*Dubrovsky*	Patrick Neate
Alexander Pushkin	*Ruslan and Lyudmila*	Colm Tóibín
François Rabelais	*Pantagruel*	Paul Bailey
François Rabelais	*Gargantua*	Paul Bailey
Christina Rossetti	*Commonplace*	Andrew Motion
George Sand	*The Devil's Pool*	Victoria Glendinning
Jean-Paul Sartre	*The Wall*	Justin Cartwright
Friedrich von Schiller	*The Ghost-seer*	Martin Jarvis
Mary Shelley	*Transformation*	
Percy Bysshe Shelley	*Zastrozzi*	Germaine Greer
Stendhal	*Memoirs of an Egotist*	Doris Lessing
Robert Louis Stevenson	*Dr Jekyll and Mr Hyde*	Helen Dunmore
Theodor Storm	*The Lake of the Bees*	Alan Sillitoe
Leo Tolstoy	*The Death of Ivan Ilych*	
Leo Tolstoy	*Hadji Murat*	Colm Tóibín
Ivan Turgenev	*Faust*	Simon Callow
Mark Twain	*The Diary of Adam and Eve*	John Updike
Mark Twain	*Tom Sawyer, Detective*	
Oscar Wilde	*The Portrait of Mr W.H.*	Peter Ackroyd
Virginia Woolf	*Carlyle's House and Other Sketches*	Doris Lessing
Virginia Woolf	*Monday or Tuesday*	Scarlett Thomas
Emile Zola	*For a Night of Love*	A.N. Wilson